AUTOMATIC WRITING

and

AUTOMATISM IN ART

Peter Preston

Illuminatus Press

Peter Preston has asserted his right under the Copyright, Designs and
Patents Act, 1988, to be identified as the author of this book.

First Edition printed 2022

ISBN 9798406983300

Published by
Illuminatus Press

CONTENTS

continued

CONTENTS continued

Other Books

A Matter of Time
(Short Stories)

Inner Thoughts Outer Spaces
(Monologues and Sketches)

The Divine Undiscovered
(Poetry Collection)

Going Through Stages
(Autobiography)

Introduction

First and foremost, my account of the events that began in May 1989 makes no claims about the origins of the material. I did not search for or deliberately attempt to make any sort of contact with any paranormal entities to produce the messages. They were thrust upon me with no warning whatsoever but as time passed, I became sensitive to the impulse that alerted me that something was afoot. It is only now, some 32 years later, that I have felt able to tell the story of a period in my life that was absolutely real from my point of view. This book, therefore, is partly autobiographical in nature. In addition, I have tried to acquaint the reader with an overall understanding and history of the phenomenon, including a look at some of the outstanding exponents and personalities who have come to the fore.

I have endeavoured to match the transcriptions as near as possible to the original writings and only added the minimum of punctuation to aid readability. The reader will find grammatical anomalies with words such as there / their etc because the context of some words was not understood in isolation. The date and time of each message was added afterwards and not during the actual session, the duration of which is nigh on impossible to determine. In fact, I read some of the later writings for the first time during the preparation of this book.

Certainly, some of the writing styles bear no resemblance to my own and the references to any form of god do not resonate with my own views on faith and religion. The secular approach to spirituality that may be observed in the texts does concur with my belief in the universal brotherhood of mankind but this is not unreasonable in view of the connection that was established.

I have also included some of my other experiences that are related to the writings. They occurred during the period of seven years when my sensitivity was at its height. These incidents and the main messages themselves have been offered for you to decide from whence they emanated, how they came about, and what, if anything, they actually mean.

Peter Preston - January 2022

What is Automatic Writing?

Since the beginning of civilisation, the human race has had a fascination with the concept of life after death and been inquisitive about the relationship between the two realms. They have been curious to communicate with the spirits from the other side, particularly after the recent loss of a loved one. Automatic writing evolved as a means by which mediums and ordinary people could receive psychic messages from the spirit world. In Victorian times, there was a huge surge of interest in the occult spheres of Spiritualism, Surrealism and spirit-communication, especially in the wake of World War 1.

Automatic writing, also known as spirit writing, inspired writing, or trance writing, is a form of psychography and is not an exact science. It is a much closer bedfellow to psychology and philosophy, wherein it may be possible to find a route through to an explanation that satisfies the enquiring mind. However, for the person upon whom automatic writing has been bestowed, it is likely that each will have his or her own interpretation of the phenomenon, from whence it emanates, and whether or not it has some deeper personal meaning for them.

It is very easy for sceptics to dismiss automatic writing as nonsense in the same way that people will scoff at the idea of believing in ghosts. They may consider it absurd that the spirits of dead people are so weary of the afterlife that they send messages to anyone prepared to listen and write them down. They may ask for scientific proof that the messages originate from a world of spirit or that they offer any sort of proof of the survival of human personality after bodily death. They may also ridicule or denigrate practitioners who genuinely and sincerely receive automatic writing in good faith. The word faith is important here. Most religious people in the world are monotheistic and believe in one supreme god. Their principal object of faith is accepted as being omnipotent, omniscient, omnipresent, and eternal. Some other types of religion are based on polytheism, the belief in multiple deities. In these or any other religious beliefs such as pantheism and autotheism, faith is the fundamental factor. Adherents of atheism or agnosticism base their beliefs in the non-existence of God. There is no scientific proof that a god in any shape or form actually exists yet millions of people readily accept the existence of a supreme being without question. It is all about one's faith and beliefs. Therefore, it is surely inequitable to dismiss paranormal activity such as automatic writing as being any less valid than religious belief. It is not reasonable to dismiss a concept just because it does not suit the preferences of the viewer. If one is responsive to one belief structure without scientific explanation then surely this acceptance can be applied to other forms of spiritist activity. Telepathy, Spiritualism, and the devotees of ghost hunting, ufology, and cryptozoology all have a part to play in a greater understanding of the human psyche and subconscious.

Automatic writing should not be confused with 'free writing' or 'asemic writing'. One of the early pioneers of free writing was the Chicago born writer and associate editor of *The American Review*, Dorothea Brande (1893–1948). Her book *Becoming a Writer* (1934) advised people to write as fast as they could for thirty minutes every morning as a preliminary to assembling a more structured and meaningful text later.

The freeing up of the thought processes without consideration for grammar, spelling, or consistency of topic often produces abstract and garbled results but it can help writers to overcome writing blocks and lack of confidence. Writers are instructed to jot down whatever springs to mind and if nothing is forthcoming, then just writing random words or phrases until another idea is found. People can scribble about their inability to produce anything or about their frustration at not being able to do so. Anything goes just so long as the pen keeps moving and that the words on the paper are not examined until the end of the session.

Peter Elbow refers to freewriting in his book *Writing Without Teachers* (1973), as does Julia Cameron in *The Artist's Way* (1992).

Nowadays, teachers in creative writing classes often encourage their students to practice free writing for a set time as part of a daily routine.

The computer age has even brought us 'freeblogging' where the writer types continuously instead of using pen and paper. This technique should not be confused with another use of the word that describes the process of reblogging another person's blog posting instead of creating their own.

Asemic writing, first coined by the visual poets Tim Gaze and Jim Leftwich in 1997, is much more difficult to define in view of the many philosophies and styles that make up this hybrid art form. The word asemic means 'the absence of semantic meaning' and people who produce such works normally consider themselves to be artists more than writers. Lines and symbols may appear to form words but as these are not related to any particular meaning, they can be treated in the same way as abstract art where all interpretations are equally persuasive on any level. The work, therefore, can cross linguistic boundaries and have limitless meanings, no meaning at all, or change and develop over time. It can be made manifest by flowing as a stream of consciousness or be created intentionally but it is typically considered to be an enjoyable experience. The interpretation of it is open-ended and relies as much on the experience of its creation as it does on the viewer's perception of the finished work and, in some ways, the reader or viewer is a joint creator of the work. Nearly everyone unknowingly produces a simple form of asemic writing although it may not be necessarily be classed as artistic. It can be as simple as testing a pen or semi-constructive in the form of doodling.

When one first encounters the paranormal or someone who claims first-hand experience of the subject, there is a responsibility to decide on both the credulity and integrity of the reporter. The world of psychical matters abounds with the misguided, the gullible, but worst of all, the charlatan. Over the years, I have encountered quite a few charlatans on my journey through the fields of mind, body, and spirit. I don't condemn the accidental charlatan who, by means of self-delusion or relentless wish-fulfilment, finds their views and products presented to all and sundry. However, there is no place for the bogus and phoney operators in the world of spirit, where they may take advantage of the unwary but genuinely sincere seekers of revelation. It is no surprise, therefore, that like any other paranormal subject, automatic writing can fall victim to the hoaxer or people looking to gain an advantage from their actions. This action can be, and frequently is, for financial gain but can just as easily be for reasons of self-glorification.

The Merriam-Webster dictionary defines it as 'writing produced without conscious intention as if of telepathic or spiritualistic origin'. The Collins Dictionary defines it as 'writing performed without apparent intent or conscious control, especially to achieve spontaneity or uncensored expression'.

It is interesting to note that in neither case do these respected publications mention it as a 'claimed' ability although some other noteworthy institutions do define it as such. This does indicate a partial acceptance that automatic writings can be of a genuine nature and not some artificially contrived event. By its very nature, the process involves the production of writing without the use of the conscious mind. The writer does not necessarily have to be in any particular state of mind during the process. They may be awake normally in recognisable surroundings or in a state of trance or semi-trance but invariably they are not aware or focused upon the actions or results of their writing hand. It is generally accepted that people have produced writings that are not in keeping with the material they would normally generate when they are only employing their conscious mind and that they are able to write with authority on matters normally outside their own knowledge. In addition, the writing thus created may be noticeably different when compared with their normal handwriting.

The receipt of communications from well-known but deceased authors is not uncommon and is a particular case in point. Critics will denigrate posthumous works as being mediocre compared to an author's output during his or her lifetime. However, one should expect the new works to be inferior

10

to some degree. The information, whether it has been received spiritually or derived from the subconscious, has been translated by a living person whose own intellect may differ markedly from the original writer. The source of these writings is the main bone of contention and the area most questioned by sceptics, especially in the area of Spiritualism. They assert that the messages originate in the subconscious mind and that there is nothing to support the belief that they have supernatural origins. Critics also quote the ideomotor effect, a term first used by William Benjamin Carpenter in a scientific paper in 1852. Carpenter proposed that the results of a Ouija board could be explained by a subject making movements without a conscious decision to take action. This is commonly displayed in the body's reflexive response to pain for example, and in the spontaneous production of tears at a time of emotional stimulus. In fact, many subjects are unmoved by such doubts and do not believe that the events originate wholly from within their own self and sphere of influence. This has led some researchers to come to the conclusion that 'honest, intelligent people can unconsciously engage in muscular activity that is consistent with their expectations'.

The occurrence of automatic writing is often a product of Spiritualism and séances but the New Age movements that had their birth in the 1970s also used the process as a means of channelling spirits from beyond the veil. Early communications were inefficient and consisted of knocks and raps but the increased acceptance and enthusiasm for automatic writing produced quicker results in the attempts to receive messages from 'the other side'. Early attempts at producing writings were made using a pencil secured to a basket or a planchette but mediums soon began to accept that holding the pen or pencil in the hand was the best approach to producing any sort of legible message. In more modern times, automatic writing might involve typewriters and computers but in all cases the channelling is of a voluntary nature and should be differentiated from possession where the subjects have no control over their actions.

The use of automatic writing as an alternative therapy is disputed and its value in psychotherapy is questioned owing to the lack of scientific evidence. However, it has been used in Freudian psychoanalysis in order to access the deeper recesses of the human mind. Sigmund Freud (1856–1939) himself explored various techniques to reveal the subconscious thoughts of his patients, including automatic writing or drawing. Some sceptics are of the opinion that a writer's unconscious thoughts are no more insightful than their conscious ones as it is impossible to determine where the true self exists.

The 19th century French psychologist Pierre Janet (1859–1947) thought that automatic writing was a form of somnambulism and he viewed hypnosis and multiple personality syndrome in the same way.

The American psychologist Anita Mühl (1886–1952) thought that automatic writing lay in the 'paraconscious' which was perceived to be an area where images and thoughts could be recalled into a state of awareness without too much difficulty. In her book *Automatic Writing* (1930), she considered that automatic writing may be beneficial in the study of certain mental illnesses by revealing the make-up of the personality.

Although this book is primarily concerned with automatic writing, the phenomenon is also manifest in other forms of expression. The process of automatic drawing or painting is a very similar experience. Automatic drawing is performed by the subject freeing themselves of the conscious control of the hand and allowing random marks to form on the paper or other medium. The resulting image may be attributed partly to the subconscious although, as in automatic writing, some physicality of the subject must be contributing to the final result, even if there is no intention to do so. Advances in modern technology now allows the use of computers to create automatic drawing. Another fascinating and equally important area of channelled communication relates to the performance of music and musical notation. Although I have not encountered these artistic and musical forms of automatism personally, they are fascinating subjects. The main thrust of this book is to do with automatic writing but I have included references to some notable artists who have been influenced by automatism.

No book of this kind can ever include every aspect of its subject, therefore readers may feel that a particular person has been omitted. In addition, the short biographies of people do not necessarily do justice to their lives but they do invite the reader to research them in more detail elsewhere.

Many people throughout history have received channelled material in several different forms and each of them has their own unique place in the human experience. Sometimes, mediums with little artistic ability will feel the urge to draw or paint and yet produce artworks way beyond their normal standard and, in some cases, in the style of a famous artist.

In the future, automatic writing may yet prove to be a valuable tool in the search for a better understanding of the conscious and unconscious elements of the human mind. It may also contribute to finding an answer to the impenetrable question of whether or not there is survival of the spirit after bodily death.

The Early History

Automatic writing is not a modern phenomenon or fad. It has a very long tradition in China where its origins may be traced back as far as the Liu Song Dynasty (420–479). It was originally called spirit writing, when a suspended sieve or winnowing tray was used by mediums to receive messages from various deities and spirits.

It was further developed during the Tang dynasty (618–907) although it did not become popular until the Song Dynasty (960–1279) when writers such as Su Shi and Shen Kuo associated its beginnings with summoning the Spirit of the Latrine, Zigu or 'Purple Maiden'.

The advent of the Ming dynasty (1368–1644) saw it become known as Fuji or Fu Chi. Fuji made use of a planchette whereby a stick, usually made from peach or willow, would be caused to write Chinese characters in incense, ashes or sand. The Fuji method was very close to the way that planchette writing is produced in the modern day except in olden times, the whole ceremony was very formal and followed strict conventions using familiar participants. A Pingsha was responsible for smoothing out the shapan or sand table. Two people, called Jishou, would hold the sieve or planchette although only one of them is supposedly possessed by a spirit known as a xian or shen. A Dujizhe interpreted the letters and the Chaojizhe made a record of them. The texts produced through Fuji spirit writing were known as Jiwen. The practice flourished and the Jiajing Emperor, who reigned from 1521 to 1567, constructed a planchette altar or jitan in the Forbidden City at the centre of what is now Beijing.

In the 1890s, messages received through spirit writing led to the foundation of several Chinese salvationist religions.

The Qing Dynasty (1644–1912) banned the practice of planchette writing but it has continued in Taoist temples in Malaysia, Hong Kong, and Taiwan, as well as in folk shrines in China.

Fuji has strong connections with the Quanzhen School, the dominant branch of Taoism in China. Often called the All Truth Religion, it originated in 1170 during the Jin dynasty (1115–1234). The Daozang or Taoist canon includes scriptures purportedly created through spirit writing. One of these is the Huashu or Book of Transformations, a Daoist classic text dating from 930.

Personal Experiences

As my own story unfolds, I will attempt to expand on my psychic encounters in general. I do not make any claims about them, I'm just going to tell you what I experienced.

My first experience of a world where things strayed from everyday normality happened in 1957. I was ten years old and my perception of my immediate surroundings was giving me cause for concern. It did not matter whether I was looking through a window at a building or down at my hands. Nothing seemed to belong to the world that I knew and I found that it was impossible to work out the size of anything. In most cases, everything appeared to be huge compared with its normal dimensions and I found it very difficult to think straight. My mother did not seem to think that the episodes were important although she did eventually take me to the surgery where the doctor passed it off (I think) as being 'sugar deficiency'. In fact, he probably didn't have any idea what it was really. The incidents did not seem to have a trigger and they continued on and off for the best part of a year, culminating in my having an 'attack' right in the middle of my 11-Plus examination in the spring of 1958. Somehow, I managed to complete the exam, in spite of the pen and paper constantly changing size and shape in a bizarre fashion. Perhaps the experience actually helped because I passed the exam to go to Enfield Grammar School fairly comfortably. Our teacher actually read out the IQ scores gleaned from our results, something that she probably wasn't supposed to do as I have never heard of any other teachers doing such a thing. Most of the other children hovered around the 95–105 mark and I was surprised to hear my name called out followed by the score of 130. This is wholly down to the teacher, Joyce Squires, who remains to this day the best teacher I ever encountered in my twelve years spent at infants, primary, and grammar schools. Once I had started at Enfield Grammar, these weird and inexplicable occurrences faded away and I was not troubled by them again. But I had received a view of a world that was not mine, almost a different plane of existence as it were. Perhaps it was this that made me more susceptible in future years and more sensitive and receptive to receiving the automatic writings that appear in this book. Either way, when they came along I felt that I was ready for them although never once encouraging them.

My next stop along the road towards a wealth of paranormal experience was at Easter in 1965. It was only brief and yet people around the world continue to strive to achieve out of body experiences. Astral Travel is rarely encountered and is often the result of wishful thinking. I had travelled up from Enfield to stay with Rose Williams and her family prior to our wedding in October of that year. I had arrived very early in the morning at 28 Hendy Estate, Tal-y-Bont in the Conwy Valley and was packed off to sleep on the sofa for a few hours, having travelled all night. At some point, my spirit / soul, call it what you will, left the body and started to slowly leave the physical body and pass through the open doorway and into the hall. It passed over the bannister and began to rise up the stairs. All the time this was happening, I could clearly see myself lying motionless on the sofa, in the same way that hospital patients sometimes experience being able to look down at themselves and the surgical staff during an operation. Just as I reached the point where my view of the sofa became obscured by the landing, I felt this enormous pull as if I was on the end of a piece of string or elastic. Known mystically as the silver cord, it was not visible to me as far as I recall although others have seen such a manifestation. I saw myself rush back the way that I had come and become safely embedded in the physical again. I only experienced the phenomenon on the one occasion but it was enough to give me a good understanding of the subject.

I had an amazing psychic healing experience in September 1980. Rose was hosting a yoga seminar at the time and the guest speaker for the weekend was Wilfred Clark (1898–1981). Wilfred, along with John Gent, had founded the British Wheel of Yoga in 1965 and the U.K. arm of Friends of Yoga International (FRYOG), later becoming an Honorary Director and Vice President of the parent body in Mumbai, India. Wilfred was also a trustee and founder member of Howard Kent's Yoga for Health Foundation at Ickwell Bury in Bedfordshire.

Wilfred was staying with us for several days and after breakfast on the morning of his departure, the subject of healing arose, at which time I told him about a problem that I was having. About a year earlier, I had begun to develop a couple of warts on my hands. I was still working in the wholesale fruit and vegetable trade and with all the heavy lifting and handling of produce, any small cut or scratch caused the warts to spread. They are highly contagious and are the result of contact with the human papillomavirus (HPV). I had tried over the counter remedies with no effect, been given prescriptions from my GP and tried cryotherapy but nothing had any impact on the condition. The warts continued to increase in number until I had about twenty on my hands, mostly about the size of fingernails. They were ugly and embarrassing and any encounter with a hard object would cause them to bleed. I was at my wits' end as to finding a solution to the problem.

Wilfred, wearing his usual white smock and the 108-bead mala necklace made from seeds of the bodhi tree, asked me to sit at the kitchen table opposite him. I neither believed nor disbelieved in healing at the time but like most things of a paranormal nature, I always kept an open mind about

15

it. Wilfred took my hands in his own across the table and we closed our eyes. No more than thirty seconds later, he released my hands and said that he had finished. He made no promises and I had no expectations either way. Wilfred went home soon after and I did not dwell on the experience at all. I had no hope of a resolution but this did, at least, mean I would not have to suffer any disappointment either.

Two or three days later, there was a noticeable difference in the condition of the warts. They had shrunk slightly and had stopped bleeding. A week after Wilfred had worked his magic, they were very clearly in retreat and my hands were on the mend. After another week, the warts had gone and my hands bore just a couple of dozen unsightly scars as evidence of the damage that the warts had done to my skin. The improvement continued and at the end of a further week, there was nothing to show that my skin had been devastated by warts for almost a year. And nothing will ever persuade me that Wilfred was not instrumental in their removal.

Wilfred died on August 15th 1981, less than a year after he changed my life and I was never able to meet him again to thank him.

At the beginning of 1987, Rose suggested that I might like to visit Jean Coombs. Jean was a local psychic, aged about 60, whose work was highly respected and so I made an appointment to go for a reading. When I phoned, she had no idea who I was and didn't ask. We just arranged a date and time and that was it. In the past, I had been curious about how these things worked but this was the first time that I had done something about it. On the appointed day, I arrived at Jean's cottage in Bodedern, Anglesey at 1.30pm and she took me through to her sitting room. Apart from being where she entertained her 'clients' it was an otherwise ordinary room. We sat down and I asked her if I might take notes as we went along. She told me that it was common for people to do so and that some people even recorded the events of the sitting on a tape recorder. I enquired as to how long the session would last and was told that 'about an hour is usual'. We chatted for a few moments and the only thing she wished to know about me was the place, date, and time of my birth. With this information she drew up my birth chart whilst I waited patiently for the afternoon to unfold. After an incredible four hours I had thirteen pages of notes, some of which were amazingly accurate. Some of the notes didn't make a great deal of sense at the time but now, as I read them again more than thirty years later, they are nearly all relevant to my life. From the accuracy of confirmed statements, one must assume that the remaining unsolved mysteries relate to events yet to happen. From the start, Jean said that it was 'the most difficult chart she had ever read'. To list all the things that were true then, or would subsequently come true, would take too long but some of them are worthy of inclusion. I make no claims for what and how everything happened and so I use the expressions just as she did at the time. She foretold of my film and stage acting nearly ten years before it came to pass. She saw a lot of boats in my life 'but not navy', an indication of my work in the port that started nine years later and continued until 2012. Sometimes, Jean would lapse into semi-trance when she connected with the spirit world and messages would come from the 'other side'.

'Your mother's mother is here, a strong woman. There's a man too but she won't let him speak. There's Willow pattern everywhere. And there's a magnet hanging in a hardware shop. There are lots of people singing 'Oh! For the Wings of a Dove' and Gilbert and Sullivan too'.

My maternal grandmother had Willow pattern china all over the kitchen dresser. She always told grandfather to 'Shut up, nobody wants to listen to your stories'. The song was her favourite and she loved Gilbert and Sullivan too. The magnet really surprised me as a big one used to hang in the shop window of The Magnet hardware shop in Enfield Highway where grandfather took his radio accumulators to be charged. She foresaw that I would have a book published and this came to pass in 2017. She said that the letter J would figure largely in my life and that another Jean would be one of them. How right she was although it was quite a few years later and in fact a total of three Js would eventually become important to me. She told me that at some point I would consider emigrating but that I should 'stay and fight at home'. In June 2015, Karen and I set things in motion to buy a house in Finisterre, France and we got right up to the point of booking ferry tickets to complete the purchase before withdrawing from it at the last minute due to complications with healthcare and family matters. Jean was quite right that I should not emigrate because the Brexit referendum was to rear its head within three years and the subsequent severing of ties with the EU would have been a total disaster for both our family and financial situations. References to my brother Adrian were not in short supply either. She saw dollars everywhere and that he would be constantly travelling backwards and forwards across the Atlantic, fifteen years before it happened for real. At the time of Jean's reading, there was absolutely no prospect of this happening.

She made lots of references to future jobs including one about having televisions everywhere. Mass computing had not yet arrived but seventeen years later, I was working in an office surrounded by computer monitors.

During one of her introspective moments, she suddenly turned to me and said 'You can do this work one day.' In due course, I was to discover that I did indeed have psychic abilities.

After about three hours, when she was in trance yet again, she began to get a message that she could not quite make out. 'They are talking about Woburn Abbey' she said but there was a lot of agitation in her exchanges with the spirit world. She eventually managed to detect that the message referred to Waltham Abbey and suddenly blurted out 'I have to go and get it. They've told me I have to give it to you'. With that, and still in trance, she went in to the next room. I could hear her opening a cupboard and the worrying sound of its contents being thrown on the floor with great haste. She returned and thrust something into my hands saying 'I have to give you this and you have to keep it.' I looked down to see what it was that she had retrieved from the cupboard with such urgency. It was a pewter tray, approximately 6" by 4" and it was engraved with a picture of Waltham Abbey church along with the name underneath. This event came as a considerable shock. Waltham Abbey is very close to Freezywater, Enfield where I grew up. There was no way that in the normal scheme of things she could have known of my connection with the place. I had played a lot of sport in Waltham Abbey and frequently gone fishing there. Father had even worked there, one of his jobs being in a sweet shop only a stone's throw from the Abbey church. It was a remarkable connection for which there is no known explanation. A lot of information continued to flow until Jean stopped falling into trance and was back on solid ground. Once she had settled, it was clear that my reading had finally ended. It was 5.20pm and she was very tired. I did offer to leave the pewter dish with her but she was adamant that I should keep it and I have it still.

It was on May 5th 1989 that I began to receive the automatic writing. That evening, in the lounge at Ty Mawr Estate, Holyhead I had a strange sensation as if someone was trying to contact me telepathically. I grabbed a pen and paper and began to transcribe the stream of information. This filled an A4 page and I had no awareness of the timescale of the event but when my visitors left, I was desperately gasping for air and I was quite sure that I had stopped breathing for several minutes. This first experience left me exhausted although as the weeks and months passed, the effect steadily diminished as I became accustomed to the process. At no time did I have any knowledge of the content and this proved to be a permanent feature of all the transcriptions. Other shorter notes followed within an hour or so. There was a burst of these 'letters' during May and they continued on and off for nearly seven years before they subsided on February 8th 1996. After that, I did receive some delightfully enigmatic and mystical poetry in 2002 which I have reproduced later in the book. Most of the incidents occurred in Anglesey but there were others in France and Greece. The sheets of paper would often show several distinctly different handwriting styles and 'voices'. There was never much of a warning that the channelling would begin. If there was, I can only liken it to someone stroking a feather down your spine without touching the skin. It was such a delicate touch but one that I came to recognise.

In June 1989, when the automatic writing was still arriving at a steady rate, Rose and I embarked on our first foreign holiday since our trip to Soest, Germany in 1973. It was a carefully planned expedition that went well in spite of it having a beginning where nothing seemed to go right for us. We left home and our first stop was at a campsite near Canterbury, leaving us in a good position to catch the sailing the next morning. It was a nice evening but we woke up at 5am to find ourselves lying in two inches of water after heavy overnight rain. It certainly cancelled out any danger of oversleeping and all we could do was to get up and sit in the car for a while. Everything was wet through, not only us but all the bedding and our clothing as well. The heater in the car didn't help because all it did was to mist up all the windows. We were cold, wet and bedraggled so there was nothing else to do but to head for Dover where we found an early morning café.

The trip through northern France took us to the town of Laon, which lies about 40 miles from the Belgian border. It was a planned stop because Laon was the medieval capital of France until the year 987, when power shifted to Paris.

We arrived there on June 19th 1989 in order to see the old town with its 12th century Cathédrale Notre-Dame. The medieval buildings sit on a plateau 100m above the new town. We headed straight for the upper town where we visited the 12th century Notre Dame Cathedral. And then on to the octagonal Romanesque Templars Chapel which stands in the Laon Museum gardens. Built in 1134 and semi derelict inside, it still possesses an excellent outer shell. It was at 3pm, in one of the chapel rooms, that an etheric connection was made and by making use of the back of a Notre Dame Cathedral leaflet, I was able to commit to paper the message that was coming through. It appears later in the book and tells of the slaughter of the Templars at Laon by King Philip IV, a fact that I was unaware of until I got back home and looked it up.

A completely different experience awaited me at the Dolmen de Bagneux, near Saumur. One of the largest megaliths in both France and Europe, I stepped inside on my own at 10.30am on June 24th and was immediately struck by a strong presence at the far end. I saw and heard a vision of a small family and was taken aback by the connection that was made, albeit for a short while. It was one of the few occasions where a short conversation took place as opposed to being a one-way transmission like the letters. The number of paranormal encounters was beginning to grow and they were occurring not long after the burst of automatic writing that I had received in May.

Four days later on June 28th 1989, we arrived at Carnac, famous for being the site of 10,000 megaliths from the Neolithic Period of nearly 6,000 years ago. Carnac had been one of our priorities and the menhirs stretched out in lines as far as the eye could see and there are no reliable sources to explain how they came to be there. I did receive two psychic messages whilst in contact with some of the megaliths and these told of the people and the origin of the alignment and erection of the stones. I don't ask the reader to believe the information, only to trust that these experiences were, for me, very real indeed.

Two days after the Carnac experience, we arrived at Le Guerno on June 30th in order to see the Templars' church. My search for its location was stymied when my emphasis on the first syllable of 'templiers' instead of the second completely foxed an elderly French woman. However, a local chap knew what I meant and directed us to the Templars' house and chapel without any fuss. It was in the chapel, just after 6pm, that I received the last ethereal message that I would receive for another twelve months. All through the times of these strange experiences, I often doubted not only what was happening but also the veracity of the material that I was gathering. What was significant though was that although I neither knew nor understood much of what was forthcoming, later study was often able to prove that the information was either reliable or plausible.

Not long after we arrived home from France, Rose and I spent a weekend with Khen Ratcliffe at his study and meditation centre in Pontfadog in the Ceiriog Valley, not far from Chirk. All the attendees traditionally met in the large library on the first evening and looking around the room, I saw that the mix of people was about the same as usual i.e. twelve women and three men. It was normal for people to sit quietly until everyone was present including Khen. Just before he arrived, I suddenly spoke without realising I was going to do so. 'Someone here is pregnant' I said and was rather embarrassed when nobody responded. My outburst was entirely vindicated about an hour later when one of the ladies announced that she was indeed pregnant and wondered how I could possibly have known. 'I just knew,' I said, 'A voice in my head told me it was so although I did not know to which lady the message referred'. Nothing else out of the ordinary occurred that weekend but the other people were a little wary of me, with good reason I suppose.

I still had one session of automatic writing to come in 1996 when, on November 8th 1994, I had an extremely vivid paranormal experience at Ty Mawr. I had been working late and had decided to sleep on the sofa in the lounge to avoid disturbing anyone. At 3am, my sleep was disturbed and I woke up to see a flickering light on the ceiling in the corner of the room. I had seen this before as it had sometimes been manifest at the time of the receipt of the automatic writing. It was pitch black outside and there was no light emanating from any of the electrical devices in the room. I rolled over, leant on one elbow, and was surprised to see that a corner of the room was now occupied by the view of a street scene in the daytime. I sat up, swung my legs round and felt them touch down on to the floor, and by this time I was fully awake. There was an old road in front of me and on the other side of it there was a band of medieval minstrels playing although I was not aware of any sound. They were wearing black and yellow horizontally striped tops and brown homespun or sackcloth garments from the waist down. I watched them for a while until they packed up their belongings and crossed the road towards me. They passed me within a couple of feet and I felt that I could have reached out and touched them as their figures were in no way transparent. After they had gone, the street scene slowly faded and the lounge returned to complete darkness. I stayed sitting on the edge of the sofa for about ten minutes in case of more activity but there was no further disturbance and I slept soundly until the next morning. There must be some sort of gateway where the house is situated because my son Michael has seen Roman soldiers marching through his bedroom wall on more than one occasion.

The
Automatic
Writings

1989–1996

May 5th 1989
11.25pm
Anglesey

For we cannot advance further in our world until you
advance in yours. Ours is the faith of all nations.
This is the urge. This is the way of all things. Yield not.
Temptations line the path. Heed not. This is the time of all
change. The way is not clear. Not yet. Only when the
son of man stands tall and true is it seen. Fear not, the
angel shall guide you on your way. This is seen from
afar. Help is at hand. Your needs shall take the place
of all others. The place is not important. The time is.
Not only others. The seal is the impulse, first and
foremost. Glance not from the path. Keep true.
There is but one true way. Stray not for the trench
of lost opportunity stretches away into the distance.
There is but one chance. You <u>MUST</u> take it. This is
most important. Many people depend on you for
their existence. We care with you. Go on and on.
The appeal of the horizon is endless. We shall
not endure lost opportunity for long. Strive for
perfection in all things. All is never lost. Fulfil
all dreams. They are your reality. We are tired.
We need you to carry on the work. This is our
greatest need. Yours is the burden to carry now.
We are at your side at all times. Do not demand too
much from those around you. Their need is great too.
Each to his own. This is the way. Our way.
We love you. Honour us. Cherish everything.
We are going now. You are cold.

      Get warm.

          See you

               again.

                  Bye

                    for

Henry   now _____
Wilkes

For we cannot advance further in our world until you advance in yours. Ours is the faith of all nations.
This is the way. This is the way of all things. Feed not.
Temptations line the path. Heed Not. This is the tie of all change. The way is not clear. Not yet. Only in the
Son of man stand tall & true. is it seen. Fear not, the angel shall guide you on your way. This is seen from afar. Help is at hand. Your needs shall take the place of all others. The place is not important. The time is.
Not only others. The seal is the impulse, first and foremost. Glance not from the path. Keep true.
There is but one true way. Stray not for the trench of lost opportunity stretches away into the chetano.
There is but one chance. You MUST take it. This is most important. Many people depend on you for their existence. We are with you. Go on & on.
The appeal of the horizon is endless. We shall not endure lost opportunity for long. Strive for perfection in all things. All is never lost. Fulfil all dreams. They are your reality. We are tired.
We need you to carry on the work. This is our greatest need. Yours is the burden to carry now.
We are at your side at all times. Do not demand too much for those around you. Their need is great too.
Each to his own. This is the way. Our way.
We love you. Honour us. Cherish everything.
We are going now. You are cold.
~~Get help.~~
See you again.
Bye

25

May 6th 1989
12.05am
Anglesey

Never again shall you see the like of me
for I am the one true light. Awake to see.
There is no end. Only a beginning. It is there for all
to see. I am another. Be with me. We are all one.
One and all.   Go now
                              Simon

12-05 am 6-5-89.

Never again shall ye see the like of me
for I am the one true light. Awake to see.
There is no end. Only a beginning. It is this for all
to see. I am another. Be with me. We are all one.
One & All. —— Go now. Simon.

May 6th 1989
12.35am (1)
Anglesey

Do not go. There shall come a time for all men. Do not despair.
3 times we shall come and go. Then you may rest. Work on.
Be happy. This is your protection. Seven times seven times seven.
This is our number. Be seen with us. Share us. Go with
us everywhere. Never leave us, for we need each
other at all times. The thread must not be broken,
it is tenuous. We come and go in your world frequently.
Recognise us. You will be shown the way. Never
forget where you came from. It is your destiny
to fulfil the chart. Go with strength in your daily
doings. You will need this strength to cope.
We can not do everything for you. You must
help. Only then can we share everything with
you. The records. These can be yours. Wince not.
Care for others. This is most important. Even the
unjust. Spare not a thought for gratification.
This is false. Not true. Only in the spirit is true
gratification to be found. We know. We are here.
You are better. We can tell. In control. Receiving
clearly. This is good. Only the few are granted this.
Do not abuse it. You are right for it. Remember.
Only the true and the wise can share it. Remember.
You do well. We are proud of you.
Do not rest on your laurels.
More work is at hand for you to do.

12.55 Am 6-5-89.

Do not go. There shall come a time for all men. Do not despair.
3 times we shall come & go. Then you may rest. Work on.
Be happy. This is your protection. Seven times seven times seven
This is our number. Be seen with us. Share us. Go with
us everywhere. Never leave us. for we need each
other at all time. The thread must not be broken
it is tenuous. We come & go in your world frequently.
Recognise us. You will be shown the way. Never
forget where you came from. It is your destiny
to fulfil the chest. Go with strength in your dark
days. You will need this strength to cope.
We can not do everything for you. You must
help. Only then can we share everything with
you. The records. These can be yours. When Not
Care for others This is most important. Even the
unjust. Spare not a thought for gratification.
This is false. Not true. Only in the spirit is true
gratification to be found. We know. We are here.
You are better. We can tell. In Control. Receiving
Clearly. This is good. Any the few are granted this.
Do not abuse it. You are right for it. Remember.
Only the true & the wise can share it. Remember.
You do well. We are proud of you.
Do not rest on your laurels.
More work is at hand for you to do.

29

May 6th 1989
12.35am (2)
Anglesey

You can do it. We know. Spare
nothing for yourself. Others need you.
This is the way. Go on and on. Rest little. There is
no time. We are of no name. We can not help you
in this respect. Are you all right? We will continue.
We are tired. It is hard work for both of us.
We are (alreae) always ready – not always able.
So are you. Go now. Until the next time.
                Good.   Bye for now until the next time _____

You can do it. We knew. Spare
nothing for yourself. Others need you.
This is the way. Go on. & on. Rest little. There is
no time. We are of no here. We can not help you
in this respect. Are you all right? We will continue.
We are tired. It is hard work. For both of us.
We are alreadealways ready — not always able.
So are you. Go now. Until the next time.
Good. Bye for now until the next time

May 6th 1989
12.48am
Anglesey

There is but little time. We are calling. We are calling.
This is the 3rd time. As we said do not despair,
help is at hand. We are stronger. We are going as the
trace is getting thin. Fear not. We are with you.
Be at peace, with blessings
                    You may rest now
                    Until next time.
                        Bye _____

12.48 am 6-5-89

There is but little time. We are calling we are calling. This is the 2nd time. As we said do not despair help is at hand. We are stronger. We are going as the trace is getting thin. Fear not. We are with you.

Be at peace with blessings

You may rest now.
Until next time.
Byron

May 6th 1989
2.50pm
Anglesey

For god is within man and man is within
God. These are the only certain truths. Fear not.
Come into our world. The world of spirit. You will
come here. You can be here now. Rest awhile.
You have done much. Come with us, we shall show you the
way of all things. Fear not the consequences of present
entanglements, for they shall bear fruit of the highest order.
Man's inhumanity to man is endless. For him. Not for us.
We see a time when such things will end. Not in your time.
Perhaps not ours. We are at an end. We are moving on.
There is a time and a place. We have found ours. You must find
yours to continue the work. Only then will you structure things
in the way of light. Teach. It is not easy, We know.
We cannot always get through to you. Be ready. We need
this. We are failing – stay awake. This is most important.
Go now. There is little time. We love you and those around
you. Help them. Their way is difficult too. You have
their chance. Use it. Wisely. Be good. Rise above
others. They need to see this light. We can not tell you now.
   Be _____

Rev. XIV.13

Note:
31 years passed before I read Revelations 14:13 and this is the text from
the King James version of The Bible.

And I heard a voice from heaven saying unto me, Write, Blessed are the
dead which die in the Lord from henceforth: Yea, saith the Spirit, that they
may rest from their labours; and their works do follow them.

2.50 Pm   SAT
         6/5/89

For god is within man & man is nothing
God, these are the only certain truth. Fear Not.
Come into our world. The world of spirit. You will
come. Love. You can be Love now. Rest awhile.
You have done much. Come with us we shall show you the
way of all things. Fear not the p consequences of present
entanglements, for they shall bear fruit of the highest order.
Mans inhumanity to man is endless. for him. Not for us
We see a time when such Things will end. Not in your time,
perhaps not our. We are at an end. We are moving on.
There is a time & a place. We have found our. You must find
yours to continue the work Only then will you structure things
in the way of light. Teach. It is not easy. We know.
We cannot always get through to you. Be Ready. We need
this. We are failing—stay awake. This is most important.
Go now. There is little time. We love you & those around
you. Help Them. Their way is difficult too. You have
their chance. Use it. Wisely. Be Good. Rise above
others. They need to see This light. We cannot tell you now.
Be ——————————

Rev. XIV.13.

35

For the lives of man are not true to the
brotherhood of man. This is how it is. Speak not to be less
than true. The fire is burning even now. Go on. Speak up for the
world longs to hear your message. We can not help you
in this work. It is for you to do. Your will is God's will. Work at
the truth as it is. Follow not paths of untruth. These are
stealing from your virtue. We are not alone in this.
Please come forth from where you are. This is not an idle
thing. Spare not time for the wasting on things. You are chosen
for this for your capacity. We know this. Hear these things
clearly. Spare not time for the wasting on idle things.
We are the light of the earth. Our time is not yours.
Work for all good. Detract not from the path.
This is most important. Deal not in ambiguity. Faith
can move mountains they say – do not forget hope and
charity. These are most important considerations
for they classify the need in man. The generations
have failed to see the need for these things.
Slow down. Time is short. Yes. But time is of your making,
not ours. There springs an eternal light which shines upon you.
This is not fully manifest yet. Beware the hidden things which
hold you back for they are not worthy of you. We hope that
this is clear. You will see what we mean. Wait.
There. That is done. We were saying about hope. Hope is
never wasted. Even when it is not supported by result.
Just as all thought goes into the ether to produce
a positive result. Negative thoughts result in
positive results. This may not be good.

For the lives of man are not true to the
brotherhood of man. This is how it is. Speak not to be less
true true. The fire is burning even now. Go on. Speak up for the
world longs to hear your message. We can not help you
in this work. It is for you to do. Your will is Gods will. Work at
the truth as it is. Follow not paths of untruth. These are
stealing from you virtue. We are not alone in this.
please come forth from where you are. This is not a idle
thing. Spare not time for the wasting on things. You are chosen
for this for your capacity. We know this. Heed those things
clearly. Spare not time for the wasting on idle things.
We are the light of the earth. But time is not yours.
Work for all good. Detract you not from the path
This is most important. Deal not in ambiguity. Faith
can move mountains they say – do not deny it however
Charity. These are most important considerations
for they classify the need in man. The greatest
love fairest to see the need for these things
Slow down. There is haste. Yes. But time is of your making
not ours. There springs an eternal light which shines upon you
This is not fully manifest yet. Beware the hidden things which
hold you back for they are not worthy of you. We hope that
this is clear. You will see what we mean. Wait.
There. that is done. We were saying about hope. Hope is
never wasted. Even when it is not supported by result.
That or all thought goes into the ether. to produce
a positive result. Negative thoughts of result in
positive result. This may not be good.

We are waiting. Your earth is beautiful.
Cherish it and its people. Fear not, time is at hand.
Gather others, they are ready for this work, as you are.
Much remains to be done for this is the rock of all ages
for man to work on. Many people have tried and failed, don't
be one of them. It is a god-given gift. Take it.
There are many times to exercise this. Be of good
cheer. The axe of judgement shall not fall upon you.
This is decided. You are pure, but watch. There are things
to do. To clear. Beware. Be wary. You are close to it.
Do not risk the blessing. Its value cannot be counted.
Not in your world. You are special we have no doubt.
Spare not a thought for needless doubt. This is not your way.
Go out and show others. Come not back to the ways of old.
It is too late for that. Others need you. It is difficult.
We know who they are. You do not. They will find you. In time.
Seek for them not. They are seeking, not you. Stay where
you are. This is important. Stand firm. Resist changes
other than good ones. This is important. We are going.
You did well to find us. We were not expecting you.
It is good. Please thank them as we do.
     Good Bye _____ love_____

we are waiting. Your earth is beautiful
Cherish it & its people. Feel not time is at hand.
Gather others they are ready for This work as you are.
Much remain to be done for this is the rock of all ages
for me to work on. Many people have tried & failed don't
be one of them. It is a godgiven gift. Take it.
There are many time to exercise this Be of good
cheer. The axe of judgment shall not fall upon you
This too is decided. You are pure. but watch. there are things
to do. to clear. beware. be wary. You are close to it.
Do not risk the blessing Its value cannot be counted.

Not in your world. You are special we have no doubt
Spare not a thought for needless doubt. This is not your way
Go out. & show others Come Not back to the ways of old.
It is too late for that. Others need you. it is difficult.
We know who they are. You do not. They will find you. In time.
Seek for them not. They are seeking not you. Stay where
you are This is important. Stand firm. Resist changes
other than good ones. This is important. We are going
You did well to find us. We were not expecting you
It is good. Please thank Them as we do.

Good Bye

May 8th 1989
10.40pm
Anglesey

For charity is not the byword of life. It is the tension
that binds the whole. The work is about binding
the agents together to produce total oneness. There is
a lacking in all men. It is your job to bind
them together. To ensure this, it is necessary
to work harder than any man before to achieve
this. There is no need of sacrifice to achieve this.
Only a pure heart. Seven times seven you may say
Nay – I cannot do this. Listen not too yourself. There
is a great need in man. Try to fulfil his dream
even if he does not appear to want it. Do it
from afar if need be. This is possible. Attitude.
Positiveness in all things. Looking back is not
the answer. Please listen. Go back to a time when
things were not the same. Now come back and see
where you are. The value you must place on this is
a great one. Peoples of the world could unite if enough
of this love could be shared. It is a long task.
Too much for one. Join with others. This is the way.
The man alone can not achieve this. The power is
too great to overcome. There is one with you
who knows. See and hear well. The message is faint.
We try and stay. There is work to do.

Goodbye for now
Love and peace _____

For charity is not the byword of life. It is the tension
that binds the whole. The work is about binding
the agents together. to produce total oneness. There is
a lacking in all men. It is your job to bind
them together. To ensure this it is necessary
to work harder than any one before to achieve
this. There is no need of sacrifice to achieve this
Only a pure heart. Seven times seven you may say
Nay - I cannot do this. Listen not to yourself. There
is a great need in man. Try to fulfil his dream.
even if he does not appear to want it. Do it
from afar if need be. This is possible. Altitude.
Positiveness in all things flocking back is not
the answer. Please listen. Go back to a time when
things were not the same. Now come back & see
where you are. The value you must place on this is
a great one. Peoples of the world could unite if enough
of this love could be shared. It is a long track
too many for one. Join with others. This is the way.
The man alone can not achieve this. The pull is
too great to overcome. There is one with you
who knows. Seek him well. The message is faint.
We try & stay. There is work to do.

Goodbye James
love & peace.

May 10th 1989
12.15pm
Anglesey

The Lamplighter movement is a good one.
Its impulse is still great. You can use it as others do.
It is not important how you manifest its presence. There comes
a time in all men's lives when the light may be turned to
but not many take this opportunity as you have done.
We love you for it, as we do the others.
There is but little time.
Care about your business.
We shall see you again. Later perhaps.

Note

I was unaware of the Lamplighter movement at the time the above was received. Later research showed that it grew out of the Big Ben Silent Minute which began in 1940 during World War 2. Following a spiritual revelation, Major Wellesley Tudor-Pole received the support of King George VI and Winston Churchill in setting up a Silent Prayer for Freedom at 9pm each evening during the striking of Big Ben. This evolved into the creation of continuously burning amber lamps around the world in support of peace and freedom. The movement continues to this day.

The lamplighter movement is a good one.

Its impulse is still great. You can use it as others do.

It is not important how you manifest its presence. There come

a time in all our lives when the light may be turned to

but not many take this opportunity as you have done.

We leave you for it. as we do the others.

There is but little time

Go about your business.

We shall see you again. Later perhaps

What is best for you. We shall watch and guide.
You will not know of it. The plane of existence
is vital to all things. Vibrate at our level if possible.
We shall not leave you. Go on. The truth is there to
be shared with all. Enter into the spirit. The spirit of
all things. Human love is the hardest lesson. And so shallow
in many ways. Expand this love to fulfil the dream
nature of things. We care not for this. The ultimate fulfilment
of man's spirit is our concern. He has to work for it.
We are not always able to be there. We try. It is difficult
to bridge the gap between existences. The door is only open
for short times. Then it closes. As it is doing now.
There comes a time for all things to just be. Here and now.
Continue working towards your goal. Never sleep. Not our kind.
We see you are going to go now. We have learned something new
this time. We do not understand it fully yet. We shall come
back to you when we are ready.

Bye for now
        Love and Peace _____

10ᵗʰ 12.5.89

What is best for you. We shall watch & guide.
You will not know of it. The plane of existence,
is vital to all things. Vibrate at our level if possible.
Be that not here you. Go on. The truth is sure to
be shared with all. enter into the spirit. The spirit of
all things. Human love is the hardest lesson. & so shallow
in many ways. expand this love to fulfil the dream
native of things. We care not for this. The ultimate fulfilment
of mans spirit is our concern. the Los to work for it.
We are not always able to be there. we try. It is difficult
to bridge the gap between existences. The door is only open
for short times. Then it closes. As it is doing now.
There comes a time for all things to just be. here & now.
Continue working towards your goal. Never sleep. Not our kind.
We see you are going to go now we have learned something new
this time. we do not understand it fully yet. we shall come
back to you when we are ready

Best for now
Love greenham

You must never give up. The unconscious mind is
the key to receiving the message. We know that time
is on your side. Not ours. You must work out the strategy
necessary to achieve your goal. Many have tried. Some
succeed. The goal is heaven sent. Man's rise from the fall
is a long process. Fear not. There rises a power greater
than any man can raise himself. You must ride on this
power to glory. It will make you strong when you are weak.
Spread your wings and fly. Man must be lifted by the
spirit. It is his destiny. He is too slow. Encourage him.
Goad him. He may not want to go. Hope springs eternal.
Light the fire for others to see. Christ has the answer.
Follow the Christ nature. It is your way. You know
this. Love is the only way. Total love is hard to
achieve. Try to show others this lesson. Spring back not from
the path. The true goal is far but may be seen.
Be aware of the God nature in all things. Listen to
everything. They all have a story to tell. We are
happy that you are back with us. We do not know
what you mean. There is a never ending sphere of
love to envelop you from us. We share this with all beings
who are ready. Many try too hard. You are not one
of them. We know. Love is the answer. We
can not show you the method. Work out
for the love and wisdom of God is available to
all men who would open themselves.

You must never give up. The unconscious mind is the key to receiving the message. We know that time is on your side not ours. You must work out the strategy necessary to achieve your goal. Many have tried love succeed. The goal is heaven sent. Man's rise for the fall is a long process. Fear not. There rises a power greater than any man can resist himself. You must ride on this power to glory. It will make you strong when you are weak. Spread your wings & fly. Man must be led by the Spirit. It is his destiny. He is too slow. Encourage him. Goad him. He may not want to go. Hope springs eternal. Light the fire for others to see. Christ has the answer. Follow the Christ return. It is your way. You know this. Love is the only way. Total love is so hard to achieve. Try to show others this lesson. Spring back not from the path. The true goal is far. but may be seen. Be aware of the God nature in all things. Listen to everything. They all have a story to tell. We are happy that you are back with us. We do not know. What you mean. There is a never ending sphere of love to envelope you for us. We share this with all beings who are ready. Many try to lead. You are not one of them. We know. Love is the answer. We can not show you the method. Work out

For the love & wisdom of God is available to all men who would open themselves

47

May 13th 1989
7.50am
Anglesey

Albeit that measures are necessary for mankind's
advancement, reality stresses the need for care in the
consequence arising from such a course. Nevertheless, this
course is indicated in a most profound way. The time has
come for all men to work at his path even in a small way,
regardless of how small. Never forget the lessons. These are most
important. Shelving the great plan does not work for it
passes by those who resist it. Let it in and shine
its light. You will be rewarded by this move towards
joining heaven and earth. Greatly. See how time does its
noble work for good of all. Speak only to those who
tune in correctly. Tread carefully with those who
speak against the true way. Their way is their way.
Spare not a thought for them for they damage the
etheric envelope of your existence. This is most
important. We contact you today just to tell you this.
You will not recognise them easily for they become
veiled in your sight. Not in ours. There is a distraction.
There, that is better. The right time is the right time
for all things. It is going. Too much too late. There.

Speak not for the truth of other men's sights. It is a
dead end for them. We free you from this bondage
to us at the present time. We are going.

    Bye for now
                 – love to all mankind

Albeit that measures are necessary for mankinds advancement, Reality stresses the need for care in the consequence arising for such a cause. Nevertheless, this cause is indicated in a most profound way. The time has come for all man to work at his path even in a small way regardless of how small. Never forget the lessons. These are most important, showing the great plan does not work for it passes by those who resist it. Let it in & shine its light. You will be rewarded by this move forwards joining heaven & earth. greatly. See how this does its noble work for good of all. Speak only to those who tune in correctly. Tread carefully with those who speak against the true way. Their way is their way.

Spare not a thought for them for they damage the etheric envelope of your existence. This is most important. We contact you today just to tell you this. You will not recognise them easily for they become veiled in your sight. Not in ours. There is a displeasure. There that is better. The right time in the right time for all things. It is gone. too much too late. There. Speak not for the truth of other mans sights. it is a deadend. for them. We free you from this bondage — to act at the present time. We are going.

Bye for now — love to all naked.

49

May 18th 1989
10.40am
Anglesey

For until the mind is of the spirit it can not dwelleth
in the house of the Lord. This we know. This is not
that we do not care for those who are not of your persuasion.
We love all those who would walk the path. There is no way
that – love conquers all. The shell of man's development
is but a small obstacle to us. Wherein (is) we may see delight in
man's spiritual success. We see you are back with us. This is good.
The sweet smell of . . . . is filtering through. This is not working.
Return – we shall come with you. Open the gate for us.
Rewards await those who share with us the glory of man's passing.
Spare not a thought for sensation. Live in the spirit. This is the
only way. We know. Go. help is at hand. Love is everything.
The union must be pure. This is the work. Go.
    Bye for now. _____

For until the mind is of the spirit it can not dwelleth in the house of the lord. This we know. Think not that we do not care for those who are not of your persuasion. We love all those who would walk the path. There is no way but — love conquers all. The shell of mans development is but a small obstacle to us. When in we may see delight in mans spiritual success. We see you are back into in. This is good. The sweet smell of .... is felting though. This is not working.

Return — we shall come with you. Open the gate for us. Rewards await those who show unto is the glory of mans passing. Spare not a thought for sensation. Live in the spirit. This is the only way. We know. Go. Help is at hand. Love is everything. The umain must be pure. This is the work. Go.

Bye for now. —

May 27th 1989
12 Noon (1)
Anglesey

For man's life shall not be truly found in the
hedgerows of life. No, this gap twixt heaven and earth is
not to be found in this quarter. Many times life has passed by
those who would not see. The splendour and glory of that
which is lost is incomprehensible to those to whom it seems not
to matter. We channel through you. To tell the world of this
divine mission. Not yours. Everyone must play their part.
Fear not that the responsibility is yours alone. This is not so.
Man must drop his disguise to achieve eternal
[telephone rings but is not answered]
brotherhood. They seek far and wide for the treasure that lies within.
Here is the jewel from the holiest temple to be found. Man has great
uncharted depths that he may be occasionally allowed to see. It is
dangerous for the multitude to experience these sensations. They are
of great danger when placed in the wrong hands. Even small amounts of
potency in misplaced residence can injure the spirit of the few who are
finding the way. These regal spirits must be protected while they
are growing for they represent the vanguard of man's search for cosmic
identity. Growth is not a word we use. It is your expression
of change in psychic identity. We call it gift of insight.
Be sensitive to its touch. It is always there. The perfection
of mankind is our ultimate aim. It is a long process in your
time. It just _is_ for us. We do not count as you count.
Tomorrow is today is yesterday. The records show this
to be true. You are calm again. There is much tumult. Recent

For mans, life shall not be truly found in the regions of life. No this gap that heaven + earth is not to be found in this quarter. Many times life has passed by those who will would not see. The splendour + glory of that which is lost in in comprehensible to those to whom it seems not to matter. We channel through you, to tell the world of this divine mission. Not yours. Everyone must play their part. fear not that the responsibility is yours alone. This is not so. Man must drop his disguise to achieve eternal

TELEPHONE

Brotherhood. They seek far + wide for the treasure that lies within. Here is the jewel from the holiest temple to be found. Man has great uncharted depths that he may be occasionally allowed to see. It is dangerous for the multitude to experience these sensations. They are of great danger when placed in the wrong hands. Even small amounts of potency in misplaced residence can injure the spirit of the few who are finding the way. These regal spirits must be protected while they are growing for they represent the vanguard of mans search for Cosmic Identity. Growth is not a word we use. It is your expression of change in psychic identity. We call it gift of insight. be sensitive to its touch. It is always there. The perfection of mankind is our ultimate aim. it is a long process in your time. It just __is__ to us. We do not count as you count.

tomorrow is today is yesterday. The records show this to be true. You are calm again. There is never tumult. Recent

events have foreshadowed this meeting until now. We never leave those
who wish to continue working with us. The life hereafter is one that
many people have tried to understand and failed to do. It is not quite
as people imagine. But it is as true to us as your life is to you.

[telephone rings but is not answered]

There …

[someone enters the room]

We shall have to sever the link for a time when
peace is at hand. Be of good cheer.
Remember we love you. All of you. And your dear ones.
We watch over them too.
     Bye for now

      We are of no name

   farewell sweet wind of youth

     fly on gilded wing that we may fly too

      force the will.

events have foreshadowed the meeting until now. We come here those who wish to continue working with us. The life hereafter is one that many people have tried to understand & failed to do. It is not quite as people imagine. But it is as true to us as your life is to you.

_____

TELEPHONE

There

ROSE ENTERS.

_____

We shall have to sever the link for a time when peace is at hand. Be of good cheer.
Remember we love you. All of you. And your dear ones. We watch over them too.

Bye for now

we are of no name

farewell sweet wind of youth.

Fly on gilded wing that we may fly too

fare thee well.

_____

May 31st 1989
1.30am (1)
Anglesey

We know that (it) is not constructive to talk of moving (a) vast
amount of people towards higher consciousness at once. This is not
possible. Better that a few are moved positively in such a manner
that this advancement be positive and permanent. This is how further
growth as you call it is achieved. Man's parenthood is far beyond his
comprehension. We know. Spare a thought for the unguarded man. He is
defenceless against uncontrolled aggression from higher spheres.
We do not work in these realms and so such actions are outside
of our influence. They must be guarded against just as any
outside influence of doubtful nature must be. Spare not thought
for such happenings for they are not for your purpose.
I do not know what you mean. Yes, that is right. Not the
same. I come through for you to see that there is more than one way
of approaching the seemingly insurmountable task ahead. Go the way
of the Lord and the spirit. There is no fear on this path, only glory.
You may hear other ways of traversing the great divide. But this is
and was my way. I come not every time with others. They dominate
your thoughts while you are sympathetic to our vibrations. There is but
little time for their information to filter through. You see the difference?
This is good, it shows differentiation. You may need this. Spread your
wings. There is time for you to hear the message of another _____

My brother speaks to you in his way, I in mine. You are
fortunate that he is free to come through. He is very old
and wise in your terms. We often work together in this work

56

We knew that is not constructive to talk of moving vast
amount of people towards higher consciousness at once. This is not
possible. Better that a few are moved positively in such a manner
that this advancement be positive & permanent. This is how further
growth as you call it is achieved. Mans potential load is far beyond his
comprehension. We know. Spare a thought for the unguarded man. He in
defenceless against uncontrolled aggression for higher spheres.
We do not work in these realms & so such actions are outside
of our influence. They must be guarded against just as any
outside influence of doubtful nature must be. Spare not thought
for such happenings for they are not for your purpose.
I do not know what you mean. Yes, that is right. Not the
same. I come through for you to see that there is more than one way
of approaching the seemingly insurmountable task ahead. As the way
of the Lord & the spirit. There is no fear on this path, only glory.
You may hear other ways of traversing the great divide. but this is
& was my way. I come not every time like others. they diminish
your thoughts while you are sympathetic to our vibrations. There is but
little time for this information to filter though you see the difference. This is
good it slows differentiation. You may need this. Spread your wings
soon is time for you to hear the message from another ————

My brother speaks to you in his way, I in mine. You are
fortunate that he is free to come through. He is very old
& wise in your terms. We often work together in this work

57

and it is most rewarding on both sides of the curtain.
The splendour of the result shines across the divide
and like the jewelled star of the night. Come not to
display your words with false modesty – lest you be
taken too lightly – but let the light shine freely
with those who would care. Tread carefully for the way
is strong with temptation. You can and will ride over
it. It is not your worry this time round. Follow closely the
teaching you have chosen. You know better than others.
Follow the heart but with care. I am going. There is another.

Fill your heart with joy. Life is rich with its own reward.
The merest act of living can be great joy in your heart.
This is a lesson not to forget. Many do and their time is wasted.
We will catch up with them in the end. Their time is not now.
Work together with those around you. Unity is the strength that
binds. Close but not too close. The secrecy is sometimes
necessary for those who are not quite ready. You will not see
us. We are unable to manifest in your sight at present but
we will try. Do the chairs seem full to you? It is as
it should be. We are here in time and no time. Keep the
balance and the contact may be held. Spiritual
enlightenment is harder than the earthly kind. Man may be
taught but he may not always learn. This problem
is always hard to overcome.

& it is most rewarding on both sides of the curtain. The splendour of the result shines across the divide & like the jewelled star of the night ____ come not to display your wares with false modesty — lest you be ~~taken too lightly~~ — but let the light shine freely with those who would care. Tread carefully for the way is strong with temptation. You can & will ride over it. It is not your worry this time round. Follow closely the teaching you have chosen. You know better than others follow the heart but with care. I am going. There is another.

Fill your heart with joy. Life is rich with its own reward. The merest act of living can be great joy in your heart. This is a lesson not to forget. Many do & their time is wasted. We will catch up with them in the end. There time is not now. Work together with those around you. Unity is the strength that binds. Close but not ~~too~~ close. The secrecy is sometimes necessary for those who are not quite ready. You will not see us. We are unable to manifest in your sight at present but we will try. Do the chairs seem full to you. It is as it should be. We are here in time & no time. Keep the balance & the contact may be held. Spiritual enlightenment is harder than the earthy kind. Man "be" taught but he may not always learn. This problem is always hard to overcome.

59

May 31st 1989
1.30am (3)
Anglesey

We share with all beings in this difficulty.
Tolerate not the lesser affairs of man.
These are transient and not worthy of wasted consideration.
Deal with one another in saintly ways.
Love in consideration of many ways of seeing.
Go in the light of wisdom and the dark of expectancy.
Expect nothing to gain everything.
Give freely that you may be given.
Walk the narrow side that room may be given you.
Treat people fairly, even though they do not know
　　what it means.
Let them 'grow' at their pace. It may be quicker
　　than forcing them. And, better.
Teaching is harder than it seems. Remember that.
This has been a longer connection than usual.
The calm nature of your settlement has accelerated
the rate of transferred information, you are more
available to open. We are going.
Bye for now. Be of good cheer.

　　We know not what you ask of us.
　　We will try and understand.
　　We love you and send you love from departed ones.
　　Bye for now _____

We share with all beings in this difficulty.
Tolerate not the lesser affairs of man.
These are transient & not worthy of wasted consideration.
Deal with one another in saintly ways.
Love in consideration of many ways of seeing.
Go in the light of wisdom & the dark of expectancy.
Expect nothing to gain everything!
Give freely that you may be given.
Walk the narrow side that room may be given you.
Treat people fairly even though they do not know
      what it means.
Let them grow at their pace. It may be quicker
      than forcing them. And. better.

Teaching is harder than it seems. Remember that.

This has been a longer connection than usual.
The calm nature of your settlement has accelerated
the rate of transferred information, you are more
available to open. we are going.
Bye for now. be of good cheer.
   We know not what you ask of us.
   We will try & understand.
   We love you & send your love for departed ones.
      Bye for now ─────────

61

For whatsoever man willeth from the body is a lie.
Only what comes from the spirit is fit for revelation.
This instinct is where the true spirit of consciousness lies.
It is to be followed with care for the ego can transmute
this information to be seen and heard as the real thing when, in
fact, it does not work that way. Only when the son of man
becomes true to himself is glory to be found on the earth
plane. Man must distance himself from the calling that
is out of his reach. But he must also distance himself from
the calling that is too close at hand. Namely, the call
of the animal instinct which still binds him to earthly
desires and gambits. The treasure is there for anyone who is
true. We have treasure beyond compare for most of it
is invisible to your seeing. Only just visible for those who
see well and are sensitive as you are. We maintain this
contact for we see you are true to your faith and
your work is disciplined and structured. You do not fall by
the wayside easily as your fellow man does. It may be
that you aspire to great things as we know you are
capable. Take time to get there and do not bolt at the
gate. Time is necessary in your case. Use it wisely.
The stones may be your guide. Be ready, willing and able.
Of all things beware. Lead man as you will but lead
him true. Show him the information if necessary but to
your own self be true. Stand by this at all times. Others
want to take over your mantle. They cannot do this
properly. The mantle has to be given, it cannot be
taken. Give freely to those who need. But beware
casting such pearls before those who would scorn
and deride you. This is not their time. From a little
seed a tree grows. Not overnight. This is why
your time is important. Your time. We have none.
We come and go like angels in the mist. Before. After.
It is all the same to us. Reach out beyond

for whatsoever man willeth from the body is a lie
only what comes from the spirit is fit for revelation.
This instinct is where the true spirit of consciousness lies.
It is to be followed with care for the ego can transmute
this information to be seen and heard as the real thing when in
fact it does not work that way. Only when the son of man
becomes true to himself is glory to be found on the earth
plane. Man must distance himself from the calling that
is out of his reach. But he must also distance himself from
the calling that is too close at hand namely the call
of the animal instinct which still binds him to earthly
desires & gambits. The treasure is there for anyone who is
true. We have treasure beyond compare for most of it
is invisible to your seeing. Only just visible for those who
see well & are sensitive as you are. We maintain this
contact for we see you are true to your faith and
your work is disciplined and structured. You do not fall by
the wayside easily as your fellow man does. It may be
that you aspire to great things as we know you are
capable. Take time to get there & do not bolt at the
gate. Time is necessary in your case. Use it wisely.
The stones may be your guide. Be ready, willing & able.
Of all things beware. Lead man as you will but lead
him true. Show him the information if necessary but to
your own self be true. Stand by this at all times. Others
want to take over your mantle. They cannot do this
properly. The mantle has to be given it cannot be
taken. Give freely to those who need. But beware
casting such pearls before those who would scorn
& deride you. This is not their time. From a little
seed a tree grows. Not overnight. This is why
your time is important. Your time. We have none.
We come & go like angels in the mist Before After
it is all the same to us. Reach out beyond

63

normal human psyche. For more information. The
way is not easy but you have the capacity.
Spare not time for the complications. Keep it simple.

Brother, I am returned. With messages of good cheer. Your
loved ones are safe with us, save one who struggles.
We try to save all who would be saved the battle
against the human will, the object that needs cutting
down most strongly. Overcome the will and obtain the
freedom to walk in the fire untouched. The search for
man's destiny is easily resolved for us. We are it. But
you and your fellow strugglers of the earth plane
are bound by self-made images of the fallen sides of
ego behaviour. That is why you sought for so long the
unattainable. Of all things, be of good cheer. A great
day dawns which I can see. It is too far away for you.
Your path lies in drawing others along. No matter. It is
for each one of us to draw our own conclusions as to what
is best for us. Not to decide what is best for other people.
But take them into account at all times for your life is
theirs and vice versa. I shall go now to work in another place.
Goodbye and God Bless You always.

Spare not a thought for false imagery. Nevertheless,
God is truth to many people who fail to grasp the
implication. Remember that it is their faith and to break
it would do more harm than good in many cases.
We leave now – be of good cheer.
We follow you everywhere and nowhere.
Call and we shall be there. If possible. The bridge
across the divide is sometimes faint as it has been.
Goodbye, Love, fear not. Walk on.
Adios, amigo. _____

normal human psyche. No more information. The
way is not easy but you have the capacity.
Spare not time for the complications. Keep it simple.

Brother, I am returned. With messages of good cheer. Your
loved ones are safe with us, save one who struggles.
We try to save all who would be saved the battle
against the human will, the object that needs cutting
down most strongly. Overcome the will & obtain the
freedom to walk in the fire untouched. The search for
mans destiny is easily resolved for us. We are it, but
you and your fellow struggles of the earth plane
are bound by self made images of the fallenest sides of
ego behaviour. That is why you sought for so long the
unattainable. Of all things be of good cheer. A great
day dawns which I can see. It is too far away for you.
Your path lies in drawing others along. No matter. It is
for each one of us to draw our own conclusions as to what
is best for us. Not to decide what is best for other people.
But take them into account at all times for your life is
theirs & vice versa. I shall go now to work in another place.
Goodbye & God Bless You always.

Spare not a thought for false imagery. Nevertheless,
God is truth to many people who fail to grasp the
implication. Remember that it is their faith & to break
it would do more harm than good in many cases.
We leave now — be of good cheer.
We follow you everywhere & nowhere.
Call & we shall be there. If possible. The bridge
across the divide is sometimes faint as it has been.
Goodbye, Love, fear not. Walk on.
Adios, amigo.

June 19th 1989
3.00pm
Laon, France

It was here that we were slaughtered, all of us.
Yes, we died here with our boots on – and our spurs.
The spurs were ringing. Yes, tinkling like distant
church bells as we died in agony. It was the king's
men that slew us. There were four of us here.
The rest were away. We do not meet many here
who hear our cry. We have not yet been
freed from our own imprisonment. Our redemption is
slow, for the crimes we committed. We went
the wrong way. We took advantage of our power
and now we are trying to free ourselves from
this bondage.

'It was Philip, that's who it was, the King!
    He killed us!'
'Be quiet Egbert, we will talk.'
'But we were dressed, not even our sandals!'

Yes, we died together, all together – just here.
The King wanted our power but he couldn't
have it. He could have anything he wanted
– except that. He took our wealth, our
possessions but the one thing he wanted,
we took with us, because it was inside
us. It is a long time since someone
listened. We often are here to cry out
but no-one hears.

It was here that we were slaughtered, all of us.
Yes, we died here with our boots on — and our spurs.
The spurs were ringing. Yes, tinkling like distant
church bells as we died in agony. It was the kings
men that slew us. There were four of us here.
The rest were away. We do not meet many here
who hear our cry. We have not yet been
freed from our own imprisonment. . Our redemption is
slow, for the crimes we committed. We went
the wrong way. We took advantage of our power
and now we are trying to free ourselves from
this bondage.

* It was philip, thats who it was, the king!.
  He killed us!

Be quiet EGBERT, we will talk.

[But we were dressed, not even our sandals!]
Yes, We died together, all together — just here.
The king wanted our power but he couldn't
have it. He could have anything he wanted
— except that. He took our wealth, our
possessions but the one thing he wanted,
we took with us, because it was inside
us. It is a long time - since   someone
listened. We often are here to cry out.
But no one hears.

MONDAY
19.6.89
3 P.M.

67

June 24th 1989
10.30am (1)
Bagneux, France

(The message is very faint).

There are three people at the left hand end around a fire.
A woman is tending and feeding an old man and someone else.
They are at a rough table eating food. She has to look
after him as he is feeble with white hair. She pokes the
fire and turns round.
'What do you want? Go away!'
   'Nothing.'
'I said go away!'
   'But I am a friend.'
'I don't care what you are, you've no right here.'
'This be our home.'
   'I am at peace with you.'
'That's all right then, but don't go disturbing us.'

She turns back to her work and I see that the third
person is a girl about twelve with dirty fair hair and a
rough dress. (One piece.) She appears not to notice me.
They continue. They live here but they are more
recent than the stones. She has some rough metal
grille above the fire on which there is meat. They eat
with their hands, the woman tearing at the meat because
she is hungry after feeding the other two and a bit impatient.
She drags the old man on to a rough bed and leaves
him. The girl she sends off. She gets up and
walks towards me.
'Now then, what's this here all about?'

✗ The message is very faint.
There are 3 people at the LH end around a fire.
A woman is tending & feeding an old man & someone else.
They are at a rough table eating food. She has to look
after him as he is feeble with white hair. She pokes the
fire & turns round.

"What do you want? Go away!"

→ "Nothing"

"I said go away!"

→ But I am a friend.

"I dont care what you are, you're no right here"
"This be our home."

→ I am at peace with you.

"Thats all right then, but dont go disturbing us."

She turns back to her work & I see that the third
person is a girl about 12 with dirty fair hair & a
rough dress. (1 piece). She appears not to notice me.
They continue. They live here but they are more
recent than the stones. She has some rough metal
grille above the fire on which there is meat. They eat
with their hands, the woman tearing at the meat because
she is hungry after feeding the other two & a bit impatient.

She drags the old man on to a rough bed & leaves
him. The girl she sends off. She gets up and
walks towards me.

"Now then, what's this here all about.")

June 24th 1989
10.30am (2)
Bagneux, France

'I am joining with you.'
'I don't understand – who are you, where you from?'
　　'I come from another time, another place.'
'I don't know what you mean.'
　　'Another time, another place.'
'I don't know about that. Wherever you be coming
from you better be going back there.'
　　'But I mean you no harm.'
'I don't care, you be off with you and leave us alone.'
　　'But …'
'Now, you be going and no more of this nonsense.
Go on, be off with you.'

Note
So I left them, not the other way
round. The first calling message was very
faint and no information was forthcoming through
the hand. But the visual image was strong
and it was able to admit vision and then message
communication together.

→ I am joining with you.

I dont understand — who are you, where you from?

→ I come from another time, another place.

I dont know what you mean.

→ Another time, another place.

I dont know about that. Wherever you be coming from you better be going back there.

→ But I mean you no harm.

I dont care you be off with you & leave us alone.

→ But —

Now you be going & no more of this nonsense. Go on be off with you.

_____

So _I_ left them, not the other way round. The first calling message was very faint & no information was forthcoming through the head. But the visual image was strong & it was able to admit vision & then message communication together.

AT BAGNEUX : The Great Dolmen
Saturday 24.6.89
10.30 A.M.

71

June 28th 1989
1.00pm (1)
Carnac, France

Why is it that you tread here among the paths of the dead? There
are places much more to your seeking than these. These places are an
entertainment not a learning process. Seek the place of the living
to develop your faculties. This is the way of furthering the human
non-level of understanding. Do not take root for too long else you
become like them. Build upon your foundations. They are strong and
will be sufficient. Likewise, do not hold back from exploring
the unknown – there is much there but beware also. Eavesdrop on
the world – all worlds – listen well, with subtlety – it is a
delicate touch – all the more so for the under-developed.
Hold on to this softest of touches. Use it for yourself if
you have to. It is not strong enough to embrace others.

It is not easy to transcend more than one gap at a time
for the energy difference is much greater than the soft
transmissions of information across the ether from spirit to
life and back again. We have done both. That is why we are
able to communicate readily in this way. The place is not
important as you know. It has more to do with the state of
your being. When it is in turmoil, it is easy and difficult at the
same time. When you are at peace, we more easily find
the point of entry. The more often you are in the right
state, the more often we are able to approach you.
Reading IS important in this work. It organises the

Why is it that you tread here among the paths of the dead? There
are places much more to your seeking than these. These places are an
entertainment not a learning process. Seek the place of the living
to develop your faculties. This is the way of furthering the human
non-level of understanding. Do not take root for too long else you
become like them. Build upon your foundations. They are strong &
will be sufficient. Likewise, do not hold back from exploring
the unknown — there is much there but beware also. Eavesdrop on
the world — all worlds — listen well, with subtlety — it is a
delicate touch — all the more so for the under-developed.
Hold on to this softest of touches. Use it for yourself if
you have to. It is not strong enough to embrace others.

It is not easy to transcend more than one gap at a time
for the energy difference is much greater than the soft
transmissions of information across the ether from spirit to
life & back again. We have done both. That is why we are
able to communicate readily in this way. The place is not
important as you know. It has more to do with the state of
you being. When it is in turmoil it is easy & difficult at the
same time. When you are at peace we more easily find
the point of entry. The more often you are in the right
state, the more often we are able to approach you.
Reading IS important, in this work. It organises the

thought processes that they may be better ordered.
Discard worthless work. It does not lead anywhere, just
do what you have to do and leave it at that. Some things
must be done – above all, give yourself time.
Time is too short in life to throw it away. You can not
always use it wisely but you must try. There is one way, that
is for sure, that time elapses without mercy. Follow the creed
and the code of life. It will not let you go far off course.
Leave not others behind if advancement happened beyond
your control. Your mind has not yet reached its limit
of tolerance, only nearly so. Even so, there is a
point of danger that you must not encounter else your
mission will fall apart. This tolerance is finely measured
and finds its own limit. Do not stretch this artificially for
we have experimented in this way and do not recommend it as a
means of exultation. Please remember this and refuse all
means of gratification that are not natural. Remember, one step
forward but two steps back is not good work. Life is but a
stage on which to perform your art. That is all. In a way.
We look for increasing contact when you are able. We know
you are willing. Be in God's way. The way of all things.
Goodbye for now. Your loving friends.
                    Abraham

Thought processes that they may be better ordered. Discard worthless work. It does not lead anywhere, just do what you have to do + leave it at that. Some things must be done — above all, to give yourself time. Time is too short in life to throw it away. You can not always use it wisely but you must try. There is one way, that is for sure, that time elapses without mercy. Follow the creed + the code of life. It will not let you go far off course. Leave not others behind if advancement happens beyond your control. Your mind has not yet reached its limit of tolerance, only nearly so. Even so, there is a point of danger that you must not encounter else your

mission will fall apart. This tolerance is finely measured + finds its own limit. do not stretch this artificially for we have experimented in this way v do not recommend it as a means of exultation. Please remember this v refuse all means of gratification that are not natural. Remember, one step forward but 2 steps back is not good work. Life is but a stage on which to perform your art. That is all. In a way. We look for increasing contact when you are able. We know you are willing. Be in God's way. The way of all things. Goodbye for now. Your loving friends.

Abraham.

June 28th 1989
1.00pm (3)
Carnac, France

It was an incantation. A channelling of energy from the
Gods through nature. We were having bad times.
No food. Pestilence and famine. Disease ravaged our people.
Other people were eating. We tried to stem the flow of
bad times by erecting the stones. We drove them in. The stones
in lines were naturally put by the heavens. That is all we knew.
Not all. Just the clever ones. There were two of them. They told us
to do all the work. They just wrote and looked and measured.
We did all the work. The lines pointed away from us to rid
us of our troubles, and towards where better life was known.
We tried to attract the good from others and send our
bad away to another place. It did not work. The two
learned more about the heavens, and our tribe dwindled
to a few – who went away. We not see them again.
A few stayed and a new village. A new life began and
all the work for nothing. It took a long time. Our hope
kept us going but nothing. We left them where they
stood. They were of no further use or good. That is the
story that mystifies you. It has been simple. Man makes
it difficult. That is all. We do not know any more.
Please leave this stone. Others are a plenty. It is time.

It was an incantation. A Channelling of energy from the
Gods through nature. We were having bad times.
No food. Pestilence & famine. Disease ravaged our people.
Other people were eating. We tried to stem the flow of
bad times by erecting the stones. We drove them in. The stones
in lines were naturally put by the heavens. That is all we knew.
Not all. just the clever ones. There were two of them. They told us
to do all the work. They just wrote & looked - measured.
We did all the work. The lines pointed away from us to rid
us of our troubles, and towards where better life was known.
We tried to attract the good from others & send our
bad away to another place. it did not work. The two
learned more about the heavens, and our tribe dwindled
to a few — who went away. We not see them again.
A few stayed & a new village. A new life began and
all the work for nothing. it took a long time. Our hope
kept us going but nothing We left them where they
stood. They were of no further use or good. That is the
story that mystifies you. it has been simple. Man makes
it difficult. That is all. We do not know any more.
please leave this stone. Others are a plenty. it is time.

28.6.89   CARNAC
Wednesday

We were frugal but plentiful here. We all
survived here unlike many of our brothers. Horses.
We heard horses. Never saw them. The people were good.
They had learned our ways. We were true to our work. We
deserved to live. We moved in the truth of our being.
Our awareness steeped in the tradition of our order.
We protected the man who would journey in search of his soul.
It was good work but dangerous. How many came and went in
the name of the lord. How many. We could not count them.
They lived and died on the road. The faces often white
with fear, torn from hunger and the reduced position of
being unable to fend for themselves. We thought nothing
of our work. It was our faith. We strengthened the path of
Christian unity by our presence. How we shone in the
sunlight. Our robes often covered in the blood of others.
Often our own. It was a wintry day that time came.
A ploughed field. A thorny hedge. The last I saw.
The man who stood over me. Then nothing.
He was tall and dark, with no mercy. His
eyes shone with enjoyment at the killing of
his fellow men. May he rot in hell for
his mis-doing. He will learn his lesson.

① We were frugal but plentiful here. We all
survived here unlike many of our brother. Horses.
We heard horses. Never saw them. The people were good
They had learned our ways. We were true to our work. We
deserved to live. We moved in the truth of our being.
Our awareness steeped in the tradition of our order.
We protected the man who would journey in search of his soul.
It was good work but dangerous. How many came & went in
the name of the land. How many we could not count for
They lived & died on the road. Their faces often white
with fear, torn from hunger & the reduced position of
being unable to fend for themselves. We thought nothing
of our work. It was our faith. We strengthened the path of
Christian unity by our presence. How we became in the
sunlight. Our voices often covered in the blood of others.
Often on our own. It was a windy day that time came.
A ploughed field. A thorny hedge. The last I saw
The man who stood over me. Then nothing.
He was tall & dark, with no mercy. His
eyes shone with enjoyment at the killing of
his fellow man. May he rot in hell for
his miss doing. He will learn his lesson.

June 30th 1989
6.10pm (2)
St Guerno, France

Now I am in paradise. Not totally finished
with earthly work, but largely accomplished in
the light of my findings. It is hard to know when the
end of this struggle for supremacy over being is to be
finished but I must continue in the work as I have
been given. Seven times seven we have failed to
recognise our masters. I recognise only one. That is (the)
this one. He that shines above us. I only know God
as him. He that guideth me like a gentle light.
I know when I see him that all life is
important. It matters little in what form it
takes. That is what matters. That we
recognise that all life is important. All is
equal in God's eyes. And in his heart.
I speak to you (k)now from a distant place

Now I am in paradise. Not totally finished
with earthy work, but largely accomplished in
the light of my findings. It is hard to know when the
end of this struggle for supremacy over being is to be
finished but I must continue to the peak as I have
been given. Seven times seven we were put to
recognize our master. I recognize only one, that is the
star one. He that shine down on. I will kneel before
to him. He that guidest me like a gentle light.
I know when I see him that all life is
important. It matters little in what form it
is taken. That is what matters. That we
recognize that all life is important. All is
equal in Gods eyes. And in his heart.
I speak to you know from a distant place

that I do not know. I must (I) know it.
It does not matter. It does for me and I live
this part of life in this way. Movement is not like
on earth. I do not understand it. Still, it doesn't
matter. I go to another place now but I come and
go but not at will. It has been one and the same
thing. Coming and going. Please do not go without
kissing the altar stone. It is up at the oldest end
not where eyes see it now. You will have to look
hard to find it. You will know it when you see it.
The stone represented the heart of our order. It was
secret in olden times and remains so.

③

that I do not know. I must I knew it.
It does not matter. It does for me & I live
the part of life in this way. Movement is not the
... earth. I do not understand it. Still, it doesn't
matter. I only exist in one sense. Not so that
matters. I go to another place now but I come and
go but not at will. It has been one end for some
thing. Coming & going. Please do not go without
kissing the altar stone. It is up at the oldest end
not where eye see it now. You will have to look
hard to find it. You will find it when you see it.
The stone represented the heart of our order. It was
secret in older times & remains so.

83

September 21st 1989
12 Midnight (1)
Anglesey

For whatsoever God willeth, he willeth unto you.
It is for you to accept or deny. That is your choice.
Choice and no choice. It is but the way of the sequence.
Spare not a thought for complications.
Tis not the way of the many that matters but the way
of the few. Many are seen to act. They are not to be
followed. Like sheep. The few are very few. Always have
been. Always will be. That is the way of things.
Eternal solitude walks the path alongside the one who
would be free of man's vices. To be good is to be
different. To be different is to be isolated. Use this
isolation for your good. It will not harm you. Just keep it
and use its strength to help you sort out the tangle. It is not
new. We have seen it so many times. There comes a time
for all men. Yours is soon. Believe us. It may be slow and
subtle but it will occur. Time is not important but it is how
you measure the interval between events. We override such
basic rules. They stand in the way of true fulfilment
and glory. No matter. Earthly life is different and
needs other guidelines to complete the cycle of each
day. Speed is the problem. Nothing fast is good.

for whatsoever God willeth, he willeth unto you.
It is for you to accept or deny. That is your choice.
Choice or no choice. it is but the way of the sequence.
Spare not a thought for complications..

'tis not the way of the many that matters but the way
of the few. Many are seen to act. They are not to be
followed. Like sheep. The few are very few. Always have
been. Always will be. That is the way of things.
Eternal solitude walks the path alongside the one who
would be free of mans vices. To be good is to be
different. To be different is to be isolated. Use this
isolation for your good. it will not harm you. Just keep it
& use its strength to help you sort out the tangle. it is not
new. We have seen it so many ties. There comes a time
for all men. Yours is soon. Believe us. it may be slow &
subtle but it will occur. Time is not important. but it is how
you measure the interval between events. We override such
basic rules. They stand in the way of true fulfilment,
& glory. No matter. Earthly life is different and
needs other guidelines to complete the cycle of each
day. Speed is the problem. Nothing fast is good.

September 21st 1989
12 Midnight (2)
Anglesey

Nothing fast is good. Slow down where possible.
Let light shine where there is darkness. Let love
flow where there is hate. Let hope inspire where there is
doubt. Let the flame burn where there is cold.
Life is never extinguished in the true sense for we
know this to be true. Send not greetings to the other
side at this time. The door only opens on our side
for you. This may not always be so. There is a reason.
You would not understand. We stay a little longer
but the net is closing. There, it is done.
We leave – do not despair – time is at hand.
Things that seem important are not but beware,
the opposite is also true. Be aware of the trivial, it
may be momentous. Or nothing. We come. We go.
That is all. This is keeping us all alive. In different
ways.
     farewell
        loved ones wait
            despair is wasted energy
            channel it better

[The name Wilfred is apparent.]

Nothing fast is good. Slow down where possible.
Let light shine where there is darkness. Let love
flow where there is hate. Let hope inspire where there is
doubt. Let the flame burn where there is cold.
Life is never extinguished in the one sense for we
know this to be true. Send out greetings to the other
side at this time. The door only opens on our side
for you. This may not always be so. There is a reason.
You would not understand. We stay a little longer
but the net is closing. There it is done.
We leave—do not despair—time is at hand.
Things that seem important are not but beware
the opposite is also true. Be aware of the trivial, it
may be momentous. Or nothing. We come. We go.
That is all. This is keeping us all alive. In different
ways.
   farewell.
      loved ones won't
      despair is wasted energy
      channel it better.

the name
Wilfred is apparent.

87

January 21st 1990
7.20am (1)
Anglesey

It is good that you shall be coming here. We are in
need of contact for true self is hard to accommodate in this
place. There comes a time in all men's lives. This is
yours. There is no need to sleep, you may rest for all
time in what you call paradise in your land. Fear not
the ways of truth for they shall not harm you.
We know that your soul longs to return.
It is right that this message flows through
you now. Your contact with our side has
been fractured. Now is the time for contact to
be restored. Man is deep in his own ways.
Not the ways of the masters. It is hard for
him to not to do his natural wandering in
search of his natural yearnings. We know
this and respect the natural tendencies of man
in the matter. Never mind. Not all can

It is good that you shall be coming here. We are in
need of contact for your self is hard to accommodate in this
place. No one in pain in all many lives. This is
yours. There is no need to sleep you may rest for all
time in what you call paradise in your land. fear not
The ways of truth for they shall not harm you.
We know that your soul longs to return.
It is right that this message flows through
you now. Your contact with our side has
been fractured. Now is the time for contact to
be restored. Man, is deep in his own ways.
Not the ways of the masters. It is hard for
him to not to do his natural wandering in
search of his natural yearnings. We know
this & respect the natural tendencies of man
in this matter. Never mind. Not all can

89

aspire to spiritual greatness. For many
would be cut down on the path otherwise.
Never mind. It is the few who keep the path
open. Time is necessary for the great process
to resolve itself. We expect that many of
you would wish to be on the great path.
This is not possible at this time. When a man's
soul departs this life, it takes a new form for a
while before it finds its true destiny. You understand
this (almost anyway). Man must find his own way, it
is different for all men. (But the same). Go the way
you are on but take care not to fall too far.
You are human. You are allowed some fall. Take care.
We are going but contact is now made. You felt the
knocking on the door. Spread the wings of man through
example. There is so much to do and no way of
knowing if you are right until afterwards.
You do not know if what you are doing

aspire to spiritual greatness. Too many would be cut down on the path otherwise. Never mind. It is the few who keep the path open. This is necessary for the great process to resolve itself. We expect that many of you would wish to be on the great path. This is not possible at this time. When a man loses depth this life it takes a new form for a while before it finds its true destiny. You understand this (almost anyway). Man must find his own way, & it is different for all men (by the same). Go the way you are on but take care to not to fall too far. You are human. You are allowed some fall. Take care. We are going but contact is now made. You felt the knocking on the door. Spread the wings of man though enough. There is so much to do & No way of knowing if you are right until afterwards. You do not know if what you are doing

is right until after the events that pass. This is
passing quickly sometimes, slowly others.
Also, be on the look out for our touch. It is so
ethereal. We sway in your mind. Sway in ours.
See the way even if it is not clear. Stony paths are
often better than smooth ones. Move in the way of the Lord.
You chose that way. Be on good terms with life.
It deserves not your wrath. Harmonise with your
surroundings, blend with life, and mix with spirit.
We go ——

is right until after the events that pass. This is passing quickly sometimes, slowly others.

Ah. Be on the look out for our touch. It is so ethereal. We sway in your wind. Sway in ours. See the way even if it is not clear. Stony paths are often better than smooth ones shown in the way of the Lord. You chose that way. Be a good tern with life. It deserves not your wrath. Harmonise with your surroundings, blend with life, & mix with spirit.

We go ——

June 6th 1990
2.00pm (1)
Delphi, Greece

It is dark here and I am told to write. Many things
associated with this place are in your blood.
And in mine. I share with you the love of the
performance. I too went to places of pilgrimage
a long time ago. This is not painted right.
Try to draw more clearly. Spend time at
your worship correctly. Do not despair of
ever succeeding at anything. Live life to the
full but in obedience. Love one another.
In full time, this message is for all. Not all
are in tune. Sing and we all sing together.
Harmony as the Castalian spring gives forth.
This is the song – mix with others who
sing. They too are ready for the
mixing of souls. Those past and those
yet to come and those present.
This message comes from only one.
There are others who wait to
speak. They will come forth
in this time. Just wait. They are
never far away, not in the ether
of existence. Only in the physical.
Others are present. They hear me. Not
you. I communicate your thought through
to them. The speakers are great but
not able. This place was this once
and will be again.

Adio –

H

It is dark now & I am told to write. Many things
associated with this place are in your blood.
And in me, I shine with joy the love of the
performance. I too went to places of pilgrimage
a long time ago. This is not painted right.
Try to draw more clearly & spend time at
your worship correctly. Do not despair of
ever succeeding at anything. Live life to the
full but in obedience - love one another.
In full time, this message is for all. Not all
are in tune. Sing & we all sing together.
Harmony as the Castalian spring gives forth
this is the song. Mix with others who
sing. They too are ready for the
mixing of souls. Those past & those
yet to come / those present.
This message comes from only one
there are others who want to
speak. They will come forth
in their time. Just wait. They are
never far away; Not in the other
of existence. Only in the physical.
Others are present. They live in. Not.
you. I communicate you through them.
to them. The speakers are great but
not able. This place was this once
& will be again.

Adios –

H.

Be of sound mind and judgement and righteousness shall
be yours. Tread into the valley of darkness. Test the water.
It should be bearable – not comfortable. What is in store for
you always will be within your compass. Take heed that what
happens will be for your benefit. Loved ones need not suffer
the drawbacks of conflict. In fact, all the more they also may
benefit from the refined atmosphere of the deliverance of personal
suffering for the benefit of all. There will come a time for all men
to be spared the unnecessary suffering of each other. Go forth and
spread your wings and fly into the face of those who will
never gain one inch in their stand for their belief. We know
that from where we stand, your relaxed stance makes this
difficult. Help is at hand. You are not alone in this.
Spare no effort in the fight. The fight includes your
own personal salvation. We know and fear for you but do
not be afraid. This is not on your level of working.
Accomplish things on your level and they will happen on ours.
Do not try to accomplish things on our level only
as you will fail. You will only impress others by working in
this way. It is time once again to move on and not
leave stones unturned. I will try to be with you
at some time in this. Remember my touch on your

① 4 AM Monday 10/9/90

Be of sound mind + judgement + righteousness shall
be yours. Tread into the valley of darkness. Test the water.
It shall be bearable - Not comfortable. What is in store for
you always will be within your compass. Take heed that what
happens will be for your benefit. honest ones need not suffer
the drawbacks of conflict. In fact all the more they also reap
benefit from the far reaching atmosphere of the deliverance of personal
suffering for the benefit of all. There will come a time for all men
to be spared the unnecessary suffering of each other. Go forth +
spread your wings + fly into the face of those who will
never give an inch in their stand for their belief. We know
that from where we stand your relaxed stance makes this
difficult. Help is at hand. You are not alone in this.
Spare no effort in the fight. This fight includes your
own personal salvation. We know + feel for you but do
not be afraid. This is not on your level of working.
Accomplish things on your level + they will happen on others.
Do not try to accomplish things in one way only
as you will fail. You will only upset others by working in
this way. It is time for one you to move on + not
have stars entwined. I will try to be with you
at some time in this. Remember my touch on your

right side. It is soft but sure. Consider others but
be of the utmost care in consideration of self. Only by
this can you be sure of helping others. Neglect your
central energy and you will be of no use to anyone.
Man's great need is for self salvation. He is not
conditioned for this great journey. He is too bound up
in the ways of desire. This can only be broken down
by other's example. He shall not be <u>GIVEN</u> anything, he
must <u>TAKE</u> it and use it wisely or it <u>shall</u> be taken away
as swiftly – so swiftly he will scarcely see its coming and
going. Yours is not the way of direct intervention. Join
with others in any way and they will see that their way is
not going to achieve their personal goals. Man will never
get to cross the great divide the way he is going. I do not see the way for
him. I can only see the way he must not go. There is much love coming
across to you. We know that the way is hard for you. The path is still
fresh
and new for you. We plead that you may continue the work. We see that
you can now do this and we are pleased for you. The work must take the
form of your choosing but choose wisely. We are not dependent on
each other in your ways. But we are there in the
background. Man's progress into the world of spirit is sometimes
glimpsed briefly in time of great stress. When he manages all this
in time of safety, then he is working properly. How long we have

vyr side. It is soft but sure. Consider others but
be of the utmost care in consideration of self. Only by
this can you be sure of helping others. Neglect your
central energy & you will be of no use to anyone.
Mans great need is for self salvation. He is not
conditioned for this great journey he is too bound up
in the ways of desire. This can only be broken down
by other example. He shall not be GIVEN anything, he
must TAKE it & as it wisely w'it shall be taken away
as swiftly — So swiftly he will scarcely see its coming &
going. Yours is not the way of direct intervention. Join
with others in any way & they will see that their way is
not going to achieve the personal goals / Man will never
get to cross the great divide the way he is going. I do not see the way for
him. I can only see the way he must not go. There is much I am going across
to you. We know that the way is hard for you. the path is all but fresh
& new for you. We plead that you may continue the work. We see that you
can now do this. & we are pleased for you. The work must take the
form of your choosing but chose wisely. We are not dependent on
each other in your ways. But we are there in the
background. Man goes into the world of spirit is something
glimpsed briefly in time of great stress. When he manages to see this
in time of safety then he is working properly. How long we have

dreamed that he will abandon this desire for personal gain and work towards the whole. The whole and this whole. Prestige is not worth the pitch and toss of a coin if man's ultimate fate lies in wasted effort and lost opportunity. It is good that this cause is restored. We have tried before but you were at low ebb and unsuitable. Deliverance is at hand for all in one form or another. Do not let others miss their chance if at all possible. Times will change for all man only when he comes into contact with the reunion with spirit. He does not know it when he sees it and therefore can not benefit from its beauty and truth. We hesitate to touch some if they are not fit. Be true to the course for sincerity is its first qualification. Many fall by the wayside for motive is of utmost importance. Man's devotion must be moved away from chattels and over to divination. This process takes so long in your time that you must not concern yourself directly in this matter. Yours is the way of the stepping stone in the river. That others may cross in the right direction. Do not allow yourself to be a stone for those coming the other way. Step aside and let them fall. You can not help them. If their way is stony then so be it. Effort wasted on helping the lost cause is better used for the benefit of those more deserving. The time is here and now for ALL men. But here and now is just a term. It could be any time. But when it comes it must not be missed. So long as some note is taken of the event, all is not lost for them. Just jog their outer consciousness and we will do the rest if they are open to it. If not, that is their fault and they will be condemned to spend their life in the material quest of useless objects. It is no use consuming objects at great length if, in the end, they are of no dreamed that he will abandon this desire for personal gain & work towards the whole. The whole & this whole. Prestige is not worth the pitch & toss of a coin is mans ultimate fate lies in wasted effort & lost opportunity. It is good that this cause is restored. We have tried before but you were at low ebb & unsuitable. Deliverance is at hand for all in one form or another. Do not let others miss this chance if at all possible. Times will change for all man only when he comes into contact with the renewed with Spirit. He does not know it when he sees it & therefore can not benefit from its beauty & truth. We hesitate to force some if they are not fit. Be true to the cause for sincerity is its first qualification. Many fall by the wayside for motive is of utmost importance. Mans devotion must be moved away from chattels & over to divination. This process takes So long in your time that you must not concern yourself directly in this matter. Yours is the way of the stepping stone in the river. that others may cross in the right direction. do not allow yourself to be a stone for those coming the other way. Step aside & let them fall. You can not help them. If their way is stormy then so be it. Effort wasted in helping the lost cause is better used for the benefit of those more deserving. The time is here & now for ALL men. But here & now is just a term. It could be any time. But when it comes it must not be missed. So long as some note is taken of the event all is not lost for then. Just jog their outer consciousness & we will do the rest if they are open to it. If not that is their peril & they will be condemned to spend their life in the material quest of medio objects. It is no use consuming objects at great length if in the end they are of no

use on any other scale. We know that salvation is a difficult
quest. Man may yet surmount his problems in a short time but it does
not seem likely in your lifetime. More that you should work on yourself
that your light may shine more brightly and act like a beacon for others in
their darkness. It is not easy for you to shine brightly but try. If you
fail that is one thing but not to try is another. You must do
what ever you <u>feel</u> is right. We shall come and go in our way.
Our contact may be now more direct but be not afraid. Know us
for what we are and you will be cleansed. Others will not
understand these changes in you but help them to persevere so
that they may understand. We will be leaving you (k)now – the
power has been strong this time. Use it wisely.
Do what you think is right. You will often be correct
in your action. Love is everything. But you know.
Surmount all difficulty with a joyous heart. Be with us as
we are with you — at all times. We send wishes to your
loved ones at this time. They need your support just as you need
theirs. Do not forget this even when your needs are great. Your
shoulders are broad but do not take on too great a load.
Only what you can carry. The beast of burden is of
no use if it can not carry a piece of straw. Act within
your limits. The link is closing.

£

until the next time

F

use on any othr scale. We know that salvatn is a difficult quest. Man may yet surmount his problems in a short tim but it does not seem likely in your lifetim. More that you should work on yourself that your light may shin more brightly & act like a beacon. to othrs in this darkness. It is not easy for you to shin brightly but try. If you fail that is one thing but not to try is another. You must do what evr you ~~feel~~ is right. We shall com & go in our way our contact may be now more direct but be not afraid. Know us for what we are & you will be cleansed. Othrs will not understand thire changes in you but help them to persevere so that they may understand. We will be leaving you know - th Power has been strong this tim. Use it wisely Do what you think is right. You will often be correct in your action. Love is everything. But you know. Surmount all difficulty with a joyous heart. Be with us as we are with you —— at all tims. We send wishes to your loved ones at this tim. They need your support just as you need this. do not forget this even when your needs are great. Your shoulders ar broad. but do not take on too great a load Only what you can carry. The beast of burden is of now no use if it can not carry a piece of straw. Act within your limits. The link is closing.

until the next tim

F

The real signature is the mark you make on the
world in thy passing not some scrawl on a piece
of paper. Despair not that the paper may be blank.
This is only imaginary in your eyes. A way of
seeing is required to understand the 'writing' you make.
You leave an indelible mark by your actions, thoughts,
and deeds. These may be 'read' by others who do not
know they are seeing them. The influence one makes
is only half understood by the maker. It is SO important
to act in the way of good things. Fight on with
good intention. This will see you through no matter what
the problem. Forget much of what you read, it is
of little consequence. It is what is in the centre that
matters. The hub of your self is the centre of your universe.
Work from inside to out. Not the other way round.
Good-will out. Prepare the way for the coming of
your own lord. The lord of self. It is not always
necessary to understand one's self. It is necessary to
recognise it and act upon its message. The way of the
light is not easy. We know this. You cannot act in
this way at all times. It is only necessary to be
close to it for to be close to the light is to bathe in
its glow regardless of your immediate surroundings.
It is difficult today.
Ah yes – when you act, it is a matter of the will
overpowering the spirit, albeit briefly, this is a matter of
volition and bears some resemblance to your own psyche.
Damnation is not going to properly represent your actions
if you are not properly responsible for them. It is
the way one thinks just before the act is committed.

The real signature is the mark you make on the world & thy passing not some scrawl on a piece of paper. Despair not that the paper may be blank. This is only imaginary in your eyes. A way of seeing is required to understand the 'writing' you make. You leave an indelible mark by your actions, thoughts & deeds. These may be 'read' by others who do not know they are seeing them. The influence one makes is only half understood by the maker. It is SO important to act in the way of good things. Fight on with good intention. This will see you though no matter what the problem. Forget much of what you read, it is of little consequence. It is what is in the centre that matters. The hub of your self is the centre of your universe. Work from inside to out. Not the other way round. <u>Good-Will</u> Out. Prepare the way for the coming of your own lord. The lord of self. It is not always necessary to understand ones self. It is necessary to recognise it & act upon its message. The way of the light is not easy. We know this. You cannot act in this way at all times. It is only necessary to be close to it for to be close to the light is to bathe in its glow regardless of your immediate surroundings.

It is difficult today.

Ah yes — when you act it is a matter of the will overpowering the spirit, albeit briefly, this is a matter of volition & bears no resemblance to your own psyche. Damnation is not going to properly represent your actions if you are not properly responsible for them. It is the way one thinks just before the act is committed.

This is what is important. The resulting scenario of
the act may be a mystery to you and others. No matter.
The initial thought behind the act is what matters.
Only you truly know what this is and therefore it is
of great importance that this be recognised. Once again,
this thought is a form of signature. It leaves a mark,
however small. Do not despair if your actions sometimes
seem stupid. Remember and think back to recall the
initial thought — and work on that.
This is a strong lesson but hard to learn. We are
so bound up in our reaction to the reaction of others that
we forget that our first point of action is our thought.
Always get back to that point of creation within
yourself and examine that. Self damnation can fall
away when one looks closely at this creative centre
and you see that it is good after all. This does not
mean that evil doings can be explained away by some
easy way out. But it does help to sort out why we
seem to act in some strange way some times.
This is a new one. We have not met him / her before.
Perhaps there is hope for man if he can learn to
build on his mistakes and learn from them. Not as
individuals but as a race. It is a very fine balance
at the moment. Man could disappear – or last forever.
Unfortunately, man has the power to unwittingly choose.
If only it were another way. He has the power to
choose but is not fit to do so. The misuse of power
is all too evident. All is not lost but it is a close thing.
I/ we go now but not forever.
Give love to the place I once knew and loved myself.

J.

This is what is important. The resulting scenario of the act may be a mystery to you & others. No matter. The initial thought behind the act is what matters. Only you truly know what this is & therefore it is of great importance that this be recognised. Once again, this thought is a form of signature. It leaves a mark, however small. Do not despair if your actions sometimes seem stupid. Remember & think back to recall the initial thought — and work on that.

This is a strong lesson but hard to learn. We are so bound up in our reaction to the reaction of others that we forget that our first point of action is our thought. Always get back to that point of creation within yourself & examine that. Self damnation can fall away when one looks closely at this creative centre & you see that it is good after all. This does not mean that evil doings can be explained away by some easy way out. But it does help to sort out why we seem to act in some strange way sometimes.

This is a new one. We have not met him/her before. Perhaps there is hope for man if he can learn to build on his mistakes & learn from them. Not as individuals but as a race. It is a very fine balance at the moment. Man could disappear — at least forever. Unfortunately man has the power to unwittingly choose. If only it were another way. He has the power to choose but is not fit to do so. The misuse of power is all too evident. All is not lost but it is a close thing. I/we go now but not forever.

Give love to the place I once knew & loved myself.

J.

July 9th 1991
1.05am (1)
Anglesey

Now thou focus on what matters most clearly
to you. Please forget what has largely gone
before for it has little meaning to what is happening
at present. There is much change going through you at
this time and we observe the   that is going on inside
you at this time. Beware of wrong signals that
could dispel the myth of belonging. This should not be
confused with the giving of time in this instance.
We expect that you will struggle with this
uphill work. This is only to be expected.
Do not despair. We are many on our side and
it is not surprising that you struggle with your
unseen   in this moment. Never forget that
this conflict is natural and constant. Please find
help in this world. It is of more use to you than
help in yours where advice is distant and of no help.
Advancement is of no use if not remembered.
The above all is the lesson we learned during our
short time on earth. as you call it. Please
carry on in your best way to pathful
things so that one thing does not interfere with
another in this thing. Work as you can
when you can in the work. It is not
expected that you will become saintly
overnight. This does not happen. Just work

Now Then focus on what matters most clearly
to you. Please forget what has largely gone
before for it has little meaning to what is happening
at present. There is much change going though you at
this time & we observe the _____ that is going on inside
you at this time. Beware of wrong spirits that
could dispel the myth of belonging. This should not be
confused with the going of this _____ This is the ____.
We expect that you will struggle with the
mortal work. This is only to be expected.
Be not despair. We are many on our side &
it is not surprising that you struggle with your
_____ _____ in this respect. Now forget that
this conflict is natural & constant. Please give
help in this world. It is of more use to you than
help in yours since science is distant & of no help
Advancement is of no use if not remembered.
This above all is the lesson we learnt during our
short time on earth as you call it. Please
carry on in your best way to publish
things so that one thing does not interfere with
another in this thing. Work as you can
where you can in the work. It is not
expected that you will become saintly
overnight. This does not happen. Just work

with it in your best way. Our message for
mankind is a strange one. They expect
instant answers to difficult questions. This is not
the way of things. Many aeons must come and go
for the evolve to mature. This is not our choice
so just live with it. God's work is never done.
Just being done. Walk in the way of it
and you will see light at the end. We know
that this is not easy. That is what it
means by being important to everyone for us to
do it too. Sharpen up your response to our calling
for it is getting stronger. We call. Do not
forget we call. Coming through is a two way
communication. Not always but try for all sakes.

Many on this side try to talk but few on
your side can collect our thoughts which
must go in all directions at once. Be of good
cheer. Help is at hand again. This is
better and slower. We get through at a speed that
is more comfortable to you. Man's progress in the
world is dependent on his ability to change and
adapt to the new way of life to come.
This is not in your time. Be glad.
It is a long process. Of course. You are just
on the path of preparation. This is good,

with it is your best way the message for mankind is a strange one. They expect instant answers to difficult questions. This is not the way of things. Many aeons must come & go for the evolve to mature. This is not our choice so just live with it. Gods work to have done. Just being done. Walk in the way of it & you will see light at the end. We know that this is not easy. That is what it means by being important to everyone for us to do it too. Shapen up your response to our calling for it is getting stronger! We can do not forget we call. Coming through is a two way communication. Not always but try for all sakes.

Many on this side try to talk but few on your side can collect our thoughts which must go in all directions at once! Be of good cheer. Hero is at hand again. This is better & slower. We get through at a speed that is more comfortable to you. Mans progress in the world is dependent on his abilty to change & adapt to the new way of life to come. This is not in your time. Be glad.

It is a long process. Of course. You are just on the path of preparation this is good

for many are needed to do this.
Just be open to it. Be kind in your
actions. Be slow to chide and quick to bless.
It is an old but wise saying and wisdom is
hard to find so use well what is surviving
in this age. Spare not time for
idle chatter. But be yourself. Do not
use another's identity to do the work.
You must set the time yourself. Only
you know when you are ready. All men are
ready in our eyes but they will not change
because they do not see. When they see,
they hear. When they hear, they understand and when
they understand, they act. Sometimes too late
but that is to be expected. So much potential,
so much waste. That is the way of things.
It is part of the process whereby things grow.
Nurture these things for full blooming of the
flowers. Nature's beauty far out exceeds
man's. This is not unusual to your side.
Just work with it. Please send love
to loved ones that listen with you.

for many are needed to do this.
Just be open to it. Be kind in your
actions. Be slow to chide & quick to bless.
It is an old but wise saying. ✓ wisdom is
hard to find so use well what is surviving
in this age. Spare not time for
idle chatter. But be yourself. Do not
use another identity to do the work.
You must set the time yourself. Only
you know when you are ready. All men are
ready in our eyes but they will not change
because they do not see. When they see
they hear. When they hear they understand & when
they understand they act. Sometimes too late
but that is to be expected. So much potential
& much waste. That is the way of things.
It is part of the process slowly things grow.
Nurture these things for full blooming of the
flowers. Nature beauty far out exceeds
ours. This is not unusual to your aide.
Just work with it. please and have
to loved ones that listen with you

July 9th 1991
1.05am (4)
Anglesey

The voice is important to understanding what
is going on inside you. Turbulent changes are
about to unfold. Gradually but steadily
things will change and stability will once
again finds its way back into your heart and
life for this is where stability must live
in all of us in the end. This has been a
good time but the thread of life is thin and
faint. We move on until our next calling.
Love to all things left behind.

L

④

This voice is important to understanding what is going on inside you. Turbulent changes are about to unfold. Gradually but steadily things will change & stability will once again find its way back into your heart & life for this is where stability must live in all of us in the end. This has been a good time but the thread of life is thin & faint. We meet once at next calling.

love to all things left behind.

115

October 30th 1994
5.20am
Anglesey

Make sure that what you want is what you want.
The heavenly path is no easy way for those of mixed
desires. We send you greetings on your plane and find it
interesting that once again you are with us. Take heart.
The world is ever a better place although it does not
seem so. Take heart. We do not try to tell you what to
do – merely to guide you on the way to higher truth
and spiritual understanding. We know that you find it hard
to stay on the path but do not despair, do not
give up. Help is always at hand. Look upwards and
around you. There is always someone close by
who can help and <u>WILL</u> help. Their time is also
difficult at this time. We leave you now but
will come again now that the channel is open once
again. Take heart. Be of good cheer. The light from
the great one pierces all and is persistent in all things.
These things we know and perceive. You can only
guess, perhaps. Fare thee well — be of good heart.
farewell _____

Make sure that what you want is what you want.
The heavenly path is no easy way for those of mixed
desires. We send you greetings on your plane & find it
interesting that once again you are with us. Take Heart.
The world is ever a better place although it does not
seem so. Take heart. We do not try to tell you what to
do — merely to guide you on the way to higher truth
& Spiritual understanding. We know that you find it hard
to stay on the path but do not despair do not
give up. Help is always at hand. Look upwards &
around you. There is always someone close by
who can help & _will_ help. Their time is also
difficult at this time. We leave you now but
will come again now that the channel is open once
again. Take heart. Be of Good cheer. The light for
the great one pierces all & is persistent in all things
These things we know & perceive. You can only
guess, perhaps. Fare thee well — be of good heart
farewell —

February 8th 1996
1.12am (1)
Anglesey

The spirit of the moment is with you.
We come not to help you with your material quest
but to guide you. We are three who sit at your
right hand. Feel us, we are here. Bear up
and use your wisdom. There is much to do before the
time is out. Go out and spread your word. Not the
word of other lesser mortals. Keep free the chosen
words of our supreme master. Keep your secrets close to
you and do not waste them on people who do not
deserve your time and energy. Their time – their leader
is elsewhere, leave it to him, leave it to them.
Can you see us? Can you feel us. Look to the
left, we are there. Look. Look.
You do not see the guardians of your peace.
They are always with you. Watching over you.
Theirs is a thankful task. They envy you.
Your opportunity to be yourself. Please go on

The Spirit of the moment is with you.

We come not to help you up your material quest but to guide you. We are three who sit at your right hand. Feel us as we are here for you and use your wisdom - there is much to do before the time is out. Go out & spread your word. Not the word of the lesser mortals. Keep free the chosen words of our supreme master. Keep your secrets close to you and do not waste them on people who do not deserve your time & energy. The time - the leader is elsewhere leave it to him leave it to them. Can you see us? Can you feel us. Look to the left we are three look look.

You do not see the guardians of your peace. They are always with you. Watching over you theirs is a thankful task. They envy you your opportunity to be yourself. Please go a

and spread the work that you have started, however
small. It all helps. It is all of great help.
We do not know how to help you
right now. Your connection has
become ragged else we are calling Mr. Rees.
Steady and come back to us. This is a very
special day. We love you. Your love is
fair and sweet but not yet flowering. Give
it time. Time will see you in full bloom.
This we know. There is a change. I do
not know what is this. Who is
this. This is an (an) new hand.
We do not recognise it.
It is not you.
I think that you

& spread the work that you have started, however small. It all helps. It is all I could help. We do not know how to help you ... Ready & come back to me. This is a very ... your love is ... but not yet flowering. Give it time. Time will see you in full bloom. This we know. There is a change. I do not know what is this. Who is this. This is an ancient hand. We do not recognise it.

February 8th 1996
1.12am (3)
Anglesey

are now reaching us across
the divide. I do not know how you
are doing it at this time, but we
are pleased it is happening.
It is not right to ask us for
divine inspiration. It would leave
your work on Earth undone
and there is much to do.
As yet, there is no joy that
we can give you that
what you want is within reach.
We will look and see.
forever ever ever _____

Are now teaching us through
the circle how we know how you
are doing it at this time, but we
are pleased it is happening.
It is not right to ask us for
further inspiration. It would leave
your work on earth undone
& there is much to do.
As yet, there is no joy. That
we can give you that
what you want is within reach
We will look & see

1.12 am 8.2.96

123

In 2002, I was given the following poem by way of automatic writing. It arrived out of nowhere and had all the hallmarks of what some writers call 'divine dictation'. During receipt of the poem, I was in what I realised afterwards to be a semi-trance and only became aware of the words when I regained a relaxed conscious state. I have always written poetry over the years, although it had been spasmodic and often not very inspiring. From 2002 onwards, my output increased considerably and the literary quality improved beyond my previous expectations. Since that time, I have been part of a poetry society and have performed my work at various festivals and events. This poem is also to be found in my first collection of poetry *I Am Angry Today* (2017).

The Divine Undiscovered

I see thee from a distance
A special being as yet unfurled
Waiting for a discovery
That is yet to be made.

What is this special power
That holds me in check
Awaiting the burst of reasoning
That defies reason.

Shall I find that ending
That untold story
That mystery that beckons
If only in my mind.

Shall spirits separate us
In this lifetime that boundaries
Distant from the affliction
Imagined in my psyche.

Perhaps spirits do not decree
That conjunction be enjoined
In this never ending spiral
Of life's eternal journey.

Shall we never meet
This life's undying meeting
Never forge the promise
Of a duty not envisaged.

When will this torment
Find a form
That once endangered
Never more engages.

Shall I live in peace
Or death with this emotion
A secret that scarcely promised
Presses deep within my need.

I dare not find expression
A certainty of emotion
Which rests in God's lap
Waiting for a found ending.

Prominent Exponents
of
Automatic Writing

John Dee (1527–c.1608)

John Dee was born on July 13th 1527 near the Tower of London. The renowned 16th century scholar experimented at great length with crystallomancy. A court mathematician and astrologer, he was an adviser to Queen Elizabeth I, even to the point of choosing the date of her coronation. He also advised the queen on the new Gregorian calendar when ten days were dispensed with to make up for the error in calculating the length of the year. When the queen was succeeded by James I, he lost his royal patronage. Dee was the author of 49 books on scientific subjects but spent much of his life in the study of alchemy, divination, and the occult. From the 1550s, he provided navigational support to England's voyages of discovery and advocated the establishment of colonies in the New World.

He first communicated with spirits by means of a scryer or crystal gazer in 1581. His meeting with Edward Kelley in 1582 led to them receiving the supposed angelic language called Enochian (via the archangel 'Uriel') and other books in 1583. It is a cryptic, linguistic construction of great intricacy and complexity, combining astrology, mathematics, and magic. It continues to be studied by modern scholars and occultists. In September 1583, Dee and Kelley embarked on an extensive tour of Europe. Kelley became the alchemist to Emperor Rudolph II but when Dee returned home in 1589, he found his library, one of the finest in Europe, had been vandalised. Although Kelley turned out to be a fraud and damaged Dee's reputation, the latter did somewhat recover his position in society.

He eventually died in poverty and relative obscurity in Mortlake, Surrey either in December 1608 or in early 1609, being cared for by his daughter Katharine until his death. The site of his grave is unknown. He was never to discover the long sought after elixir of life that an Enochian instruction had told him was to be found in the ruins of Glastonbury Abbey. In later times, the Hermetic Order of the Golden Dawn revived the rituals associated with the Enochian language and they became embedded in the Order's ceremonial magic during its heyday from 1887 to 1903. Some Enochian rituals were also adapted by the Church of Satan that was formed in 1966.

On April 18th 1873, the Anglican minister and medium William Stainton Moses was reported to have communicated with Dee by means of automatic writing. Interestingly, the messages contained some details of Dee's life that were confirmed as being correct by researchers at the British Museum Library. Modern re-evaluations of John Dee view him as a serious scholar, a competent scientist, and one of the most learned men of his day.

Emanuel Swedenborg (1688–1772)

Emanuel Swedenborg was a Swedish scientist, inventor, philosopher and Christian theologian and the son of Jesper Swedberg, Bishop of Skara. Emanuel was heavily influenced by his father's religious views, particularly those relating to the Lutheran Pietist movement. Emanuel later became well known for his book *Heaven and Hell* (1758) which gave a detailed description of the afterlife.

He was born Emanuel Swedberg on January 29th 1688 in Stockholm and from 1699 until 1709 he was educated at Uppsala University, where all classes were taught in Latin. He became interested in mathematics and the natural sciences and in 1710, he embarked on a study tour through Europe on his way to London where he lived for four years. His early suggestions regarding the calculation of longitude by lunar observation and the possibilities of aerial and undersea travel were amazingly prescient. In 1715, he returned to Sweden and published its first scientific journal *Daedalus Hyperboreus* (The Northern Daedalus) a year later. King Charles XII appointed him Assessor at the Royal College of Mines in 1716, a position he was to hold until his resignation in 1747 to concentrate on his theological writing. When the king died on November 30th 1717, Queen Ulrika Eleonora ennobled the family in recognition of the work of Jesper Swedberg and the family name was changed to Swedenborg. He spent the next two decades working on natural science and engineering projects in addition to publishing some of his most important philosophical works. He was a prolific writer except for the period 1722–1733 which he spent in study and pursuing his career as a civil servant. During a third European tour in 1734, he published *Opera Philosophica et Mineralia* (Philosophical and Logical Works) in three volumes. In the first book, he concluded that matter consisted of indivisible particles that were in constant vortical motion and that even these were composed of similarly moving particles. His ideas on atomic theory were well in advance of those proposed in 1803 by the British chemist John Dalton and he also speculated that the planets of the solar system were formed from a single nebula. In 1736, he visited France, Italy, and Holland, where he published two further great works before returning to Stockholm towards the end of 1740. In 1743, he embarked upon another European journey to research a large work on the animal kingdom and it was during this tour of Holland and England that he recorded his strange dreams and visions (past and present) in his travel journal. Considered lost until its discovery at the Royal Library in the 1850s, *Drömboken* (Journal of Dreams) detailed his spiritual experiences in 1744, including a vision of Christ on April 7th. By the end of October 1744, he had abandoned his current projects and began writing a new book about the worship of God. In April 1745, whilst in London, he dreamt (or had a vision) that the Lord had chosen him to explain the spiritual meaning of the Bible in 'The Heavenly Doctrines' and that he would be told what to write by spirit guides. The messages offered new interpretations of some of the main Christian principles such as the Resurrection and the Second Coming, and the cornerstone of Martin Luther's doctrine of justification by faith (sola fide) was set aside. However, when he returned to Stockholm in August 1745, he made no immediate mention of his 'mission' for fear of accusations of blasphemy and heresy.

There is no doubt he received much of 'The Heavenly Doctrines' by means of automatic writing. The texts were transmitted either verbally, where he heard them internally, or in a dissociated state which he described as 'I have written entire pages, and the spirits did not dictate the words, but absolutely guided my hand, so that it was they who were doing the writing.' Usually he remembered the events but quite often he was unaware of what had been written until afterwards. An examination of Swedenborg's manuscripts shows marked differences between his usual handwriting and the pages delivered by his spirit guides. Swedenborg himself was aware of this for he noted 'That my style of writing is varied according to the spirit associated with me.'

Over the next ten years, he devoted his time to the spiritual interpretation of every verse in the Bible and this dedication culminated in his great work *Arcana Coelestia* (Secrets of Heaven).

In *Earths in the Universe* (1758), his encounters with spirits from planets in and beyond the solar system led him to conclude other worlds are inhabited and that the universe could not have been created for just one planet or one heaven.

A curious incident occurred on Thursday July 19th 1759. A huge fire broke out in Stockholm which spread quickly, destroying about 300 houses. At that time, Swedenborg was dining with friends in Gothenburg, about 300 miles away. He told the assembled company at 6pm that there was a fire in Stockholm and that his house was in danger because the fire had already reached a neighbour's home. At 8pm, he was greatly relieved to announce that the fire had stopped three doors from his own home. In those times, it took two to three days for news to reach Gothenburg from Stockholm. The first official news of the fire arrived on Monday evening followed by a second messenger on Tuesday who confirmed the information uttered by Swedenborg on Thursday.

In one of his theological works, Swedenborg wrote that the eating of meat was not practiced in the early days of humanity and many took this to mean that Swedenborg was a vegetarian. The idea gained ground when some of

Swedenborg's early followers joined the vegetarian movement in the 19th century but the reports of his eating habits are not conclusive.

In July 1770, aged 82, he travelled to Amsterdam to complete his last work *Vera Christiana Religio* (The True Christian Religion) before returning to London in the summer of 1771. In December, he suffered a stroke which left him partially paralysed. In February 1772, he wrote to John Wesley to say he had been informed by the spirits that Wesley wanted to speak to him. Wesley replied that he would be away for six months but would contact him when he got back whereupon Swedenborg told him that it would be too late because he was going to die on March 29th 1772. His prediction was confirmed by Elizabeth Reynolds who was his landlord's servant.

Emanuel Swedenborg died aged 84 in London on March 29th 1772, the date that he had predicted, and was buried in the Swedish Church in Shadwell, London. His remains were removed to Uppsala Cathedral in 1908 and although the Swedish Church was demolished in 1917, he is remembered by a nearby road that was renamed Swedenborg Gardens in his honour.

Over the course of his life he completed 48 works on spiritual subjects. About 15 years after his death, the first Swedenborgian societies formed to study his works and many writers and artists were inspired and influenced by his writings. These included William Blake, Ralph Waldo Emerson, Jorge Luis Borges, Robert Frost, Carl Jung, Immanuel Kant, W B Yeats, and Arthur Conan Doyle. He never married although he wrote on the subject and owing to a stutter, there are no known instances of him speaking in public. His works have been translated into numerous languages, and commentaries and new editions are regularly issued.

Joanna Southcott (1750–1814)

Joanna Southcott (or Southcote) was a prophetess who experienced visitations from the age of 42 and in later life declared that she would give birth to the new Messiah by way of a divine pregnancy. Her story is divided between the events of her life and her legacy, which persists to the present day.

She was born on April 25th 1750 in Taleford, Devon and grew up on a small farm in Gittisham, fifteen miles from Exeter. Being a devoutly religious household, Joanna was required to read the bible every day. Her parents, Hannah and William Southcott, fell on hard times following William's persistent illnesses from 1771 until his death in 1802. Joanna received scant education and relied on her relentless study of the bible for information but managed to run the farm herself for a couple of years. However, when her mother died, she had to leave the farm and go into domestic service. Her first position was as a shop girl and maid with the Taylors in Honiton and then, in 1797, as a domestic servant at the home of an Exeter upholsterer where she also learned the trade. Her employers described her as being quiet and honest but with occasional fits of depression.

In 1792, aged 42 and around the time of her menopause, she began to have strange experiences that included dreams and visions. She received a large amount of religious prophecies in the form of automatic writing and was told that 'The Lord is awakened out of sleep. He will terribly shake the earth.' She was initially concerned that the messages were the work of the Devil and considered returning to the upholstery trade but when some of the prophecies proved to be accurate, she accepted that they were from a divine source. It appears that Joanna experienced the automatic writing with very little effort and it often arrived in verse form. She stated 'The writing comes extremely fast, much faster than I could keep up by voluntary effort. I have to turn over the pages and guard the lines of writing from running into each other; but, except for this, I need not look at the paper. I can talk on other subjects while writing. The mass of the writings consists in teachings on Religion. Some messages, however, deal with earthly matters.' She approached both the Methodists and the Dissenters with her prophecies but when they failed to offer any support she wrote to Joseph Pomeroy, the vicar of St Kew in North Cornwall. To begin with, he was sympathetic when a number of the prophecies were fulfilled but later on he considered them to be blasphemous. When he discovered that his name was being quoted in connection with the printing of her letters, he burnt her papers and withdrew his patronage. He received dozens of letters from Joanna and her supporters threatening him with divine justice. Joanna then attempted to have the messages examined by a jury of clergymen but when her letter of January 5th 1801 failed to elicit a response, she paid an Exeter printer her entire life savings of £100 to bring the prophecies to a wider audience. In February 1801, the story of how she received the prophecies and the subsequent struggle to have them recognised by the Church appeared in the 48-page booklet *The Strange Effects of Faith* and within a few weeks, she had published a second part. The Rev Thomas Philip Foley of Cambridge saw the booklets and with the help of friends including the engraver William Sharp, made another attempt to raise enough clergymen to examine Joanna's writings but church dignitaries were unwilling to co-operate. Although she was forced to borrow money to finance the cost of producing further parts of her story, in the years up to her death she published 65 pamphlets and books. It is estimated that more than 108,000 copies of her works were printed and that she attracted in excess of 100,000 followers. Joanna disclaimed any credit for her books and insisted that it was 'the work of the voice of God - Without the Spirit I am nothing'. Her movement, in spite of its being vociferous and decidedly visible, was mostly ignored by the established churches and the government of the day.

With the help of some of her more prosperous converts, Joanna moved to London where dedicated chapels were created for her followers. It had not been her intention to create a new church because her teachings were founded on 'The Great Controversy', the term she used to describe the battle between Christ and Satan. As her fame spread and the number of devotees increased, she began to issue tokens of her mission which were her famous 'seals'. These were made from squares of paper with a circle drawn (later printed) upon them, within which each follower wrote the words 'The Seal of the Lord, the Elect and Precious, Man's Redemption to Inherit the Tree of Life, to be made Heirs of God and Joint Heirs with Jesus Christ'. The squares of paper were signed by Joanna and then folded up and marked with a wax seal depicting 'I.C.' and two stars, that she had found in the Taylor's shop some years earlier. Taking the initials to represent Iesu Christi, she had distributed several thousand 'seals' to her followers within a year, intending to convert the '144,000 who had been redeemed from the earth' and guaranteed a place in heaven as mentioned in *Revelation 14*. Although she was accused of profiting from them, it seems likely that some people were selling them on for between twelve shillings and a guinea (60p–£1.05) as lucky charms in order to protect the wearer from Satan. In 1808, Joanna was commanded by her inner voice to cease the process of 'sealing' converts.

Joanna sincerely believed in her mission and prophecies and it is unlikely that her activities were fraudulent. In fact her supporters deemed that her lack of education made her the perfect vessel to receive divine truths.

At the age of 64, she received the message 'Order twelve gowns for thy wedding' which confused her as she had never considered the prospect of marriage. This was followed by 'This year in the sixty-fifth year of thy age thou shalt bear a son by the power of the Most High.' She was convinced that she had been chosen to carry a new Messiah and by March 1814 she was showing signs of being pregnant, a condition that was surprisingly confirmed by twenty medical practitioners, including a leading surgeon. Expensive gifts arrived from her followers including a sumptuously bound bible and a satinwood and gold cradle along with hundreds of other presents for the child. Comparing her situation to that of the Virgin Mary and to satisfy earthly convention, she determined that she would need a 'Joseph'. She duly married a friend, John Smith, in her bedroom on November 12th 1814. A marital condition was that if the child failed to appear then the marriage would be annulled and this appears to have been the case.

Joanna had expected the birth to occur on October 14th but by September no birth looked likely and on November 19th 1814, she had a premonition of her death and told her close friends 'Now it all appears delusion'. Having examined her will and codicil in which she had come to realise the truth, she stated that all the gifts she had received should be returned to the benefactors, whose numbers exceeded 230. Apart from the fabulous cradle, there were hundreds of items that had to be returned included gifts of gold, silver, money, and a huge number of shirts, caps, robes, and napkins.

By mid-December, she no longer bore any symptoms of pregnancy and informed her doctor that she was dying, in which event her body was to be kept warm for four days in case she was in a trance. She died on December 27th 1814 and four days later an autopsy was performed in London. No foetus was found and the doctors declared that she had dropsy, nowadays known as an oedema, whereby fluid accumulates in the body. The swelling caused by her condition probably led to the assumption of a pregnancy. Also, the disappointment and disillusionment associated with her divine mission may have caused her to give up the will to live. She was buried in Marylebone Cemetery on January 2nd 1815. She was not to rest in peace however owing to an explosion on the nearby Regent's canal in 1874. Five tons of gunpowder on the barge *Tilbury* blew up, killing three crewmen and shattering the inscription on Joanna's tombstone.

William Sharp had made a special walnut box in 1801 to hold Joanna's prophecies and papers. It was secured with strong cord, and sealed with seven seals. Joanna's inner circle protected the box and maintained the strict instruction that in the event of her death it was only to be opened at a time of national crisis and in the presence of 24 Church of England bishops. No assembly of that nature has ever occurred. The box passed through several hands and in time, a variety of other 'boxes' appeared or be alleged to exist.

Following her death, her followers were confused by her renunciation of her divine mission and successors such as George Turner, James White, and John Wroe formed splinter groups.

In 1907, Joanna's mission was revived by Helen Exeter, Alice Seymour, Rachel Fox, Kate Firth, and Mabel Barltrop, who were insistent upon the opening of the famous box and spent twenty years pestering and petitioning the clergy to do so. Helen Exeter adopted the name 'Octavia' and started her own movement in Bedford and by 1920, she had a huge following around the world. In 1923, she claimed to have healing powers and her community distributed small pieces of linen that had to be placed in water. The 'healing' liquid was then poured over the site of an injury or drunk out of a glass. Convinced that they had created a universal remedy, the community assumed the name 'The Panacea Society' and set up their headquarters in Mabel Barltrop's house. In 2012, the name was changed to 'The Panacea Charitable Trust' and the movement continues to advocate Joanna's teachings. It may still be found at the house in Albany Road, Bedford where it was originally formed, along with an interesting museum.

In 1927 the British psychical researcher Harry Price, who had a great flair for publicity, announced that he had taken possession of the box. He invited three archbishops and 80 bishops to a grand opening at the Hoare Memorial Hall, Westminster on July 11th 1927 although the bishop of Grantham was the only senior churchman to attend the meeting. There were 56 items in the box including various books and pamphlets dated between 1715 and 1796, some coins in a fob purse, a horse pistol, a woman's night-cap, and an ivory dice cup. A River Thames souvenir dated February 3rd 1814 may have been deliberately added to help with provenance. The Southcottians, as they came to be known, dismissed the box as a fake, as did historians, owing to its complete lack of material pertaining to Joanna. In the 1960s and 1970s, the Panacea Society ran publicity campaigns in British newspapers, urging the bishops to oversee the opening of the true box which they claim has been held at a secret location since 1957 until the bishops agree to the prescribed meeting. If this box is indeed the genuine article, it has never been opened.

Charles Dickens immortalised her in his opening lines of *A Tale of Two Cities* (1859) which begins in 1775. Most modern readers wouldn't notice her name but when Dickens wrote 'Mrs Southcott had recently attained her five-and-twentieth blessed birthday', he was referring to a woman (and the mysterious box bearing her name) that was famous in London at that time. Many of her prophecies were never made public and perhaps they still lie in the famous box somewhere, awaiting their own revelation.

William Blake (1757–1827)

William Blake was a visionary English poet, artist, and print maker who is perhaps best known for the first four lines of his *Auguries of Innocence*. The 132 line poem was not published until 1863, having been written some sixty years earlier.

'To see a world in a grain of sand,
And a heaven in a wild flower,
Hold infinity in the palm of your hand,
And eternity in an hour.'

Blake would probably have dismissed the term 'automatic writing' if it had existed in his time. He would have found it difficult to accept that he was merely an instrument of another being's creation. Yet his own experiences and his descriptions of the events that surrounded his work must lead one to assume that he did, indeed, receive spirit writing.

He was born the third of seven children at 28 Broad Street (now Broadwick Street) in Soho, London on November 28th 1757. Modern day pilgrims in search of a blue plaque marking the place of his birth are thwarted by the house having been demolished in 1965. The son of a hosier, James Blake, his parents were dissenters but this did not prevent the Bible from having a strong influence on him and it continued to inspire his work for the rest of his life. His contributions to art and literature were mostly disregarded during his lifetime but they are now considered to be hugely influential in the spheres of poetry and the visual arts. From the ages of ten to fourteen, he was educated at home by his mother Catherine and attended Henry Pars' drawing school in the Strand. On August 4th 1772, he was taken on by the master engraver James Basire as an apprentice and at the end of the seven-year term he became a professional engraver. He also studied at the Royal Academy of Art from October 8th 1779 but his six-year stay there was curtailed by his opposition to the views of its president, Sir Joshua Reynolds.

On August 18th 1782, aged 25, he married Catherine Boucher. Blake taught her to read and write and she became adept as an engraver and helped him to print the memorable illustrated works that we know today. Blake printed his first poetry collection *Poetical Sketches* in about 1783. Following the death of his father in 1784, Blake and James Parker (another Basire apprentice) opened a print shop but the business failed to flourish and he scratched out a living as an engraver and illustrator for the rest of his life. He published a collection of nineteen gentle, pastoral poems in *Songs of Innocence* (1789) followed by the more adult and profound 26 poems in *Songs of Experience* (1794). The two collections reflected his own complex social and political views and represented some of his finest writing and illustration.

He had visions all his life and they began when he was around nine years of age when he saw a tree crowded with angels at Peckham Rye. On another occasion, James Basire sent the young Blake to Westminster Abbey to do some sketching and he claimed to have seen Christ and his Apostles, many monks and priests, and heard their singing. In later years, he was a regular visitor to the 'London Stone' which then stood at St Swithin's Church on Cannon Street and it was there that he had visions of his 'Jerusalem'. His visions were often of a religious nature and this theme inspired much of his writing. Some of his contemporaries suggested that he suffered from hallucinations or considered him to be insane. William Wordsworth (1770–1850) wrote 'There was no doubt that this poor man was mad, but there is something in the madness of this man which interests me more than the sanity of Lord Byron and Walter Scott'. However, the most direct evidence for automatic writing comes from the hand of Blake himself. In his correspondence with William Butts about his epic poem *Milton* and his most famous work *Jerusalem*, Blake wrote 'I have written this poem from immediate dictation, twelve or sometimes twenty or thirty lines at a time without premeditation and even against my will'. In another letter he explained his writing experience thus: 'I am not ashamed, afraid or averse to tell you what ought to be told, that I am under the direction of messengers from heaven, daily and nightly'. Another letter said 'I may praise it since I dare not pretend to be any other than the secretary, the authors are in Eternity'.

From 1790 to 1800, Blake lived at 13 Hercules Buildings (demolished in 1918), North Lambeth, London but then moved to Felpham in Sussex to illustrate the works of the minor poet William Hayley. It was there, under Hayley's patronage, that he began to write *Milton*. He returned to London in 1803 as a result of a minor court case in which he was acquitted of assault and began to write and illustrate *Jerusalem*, a task that was to occupy the sixteen years from 1804 until 1820. In the mid-1820s, he produced a large amount of engravings and illustrations but his output failed to prevent him from falling into poverty and obscurity.

Blake's final years were spent at Fountain Court off the Strand and shortly before his death, he revealed that he had written 'twenty tragedies as long as Macbeth'. Unfortunately, none of these have survived. On his deathbed, he said that some of his work was the product of 'heavenly friends'. Sadly, when he died on August 12th 1827, fewer than thirty copies of *Songs of Innocence and of Experience* had been sold. His body was buried at the Dissenter's burial ground in Bunhill Fields, Islington.

After Catherine died in October 1831, Blake's manuscripts fell into the hands of Frederick Tatham who continued to sell them. Later, he became a member of the Irvingite church and this led him to burn any of Blake's manuscripts that he considered to be heretical. William Michael Rossetti also burned any works that he deemed to be of low quality. John Linnell even took the trouble to erase sexually related imagery from Blake's illustrations and drawings. The world will never know the full extent of the destruction of Blake's work and it is only in retrospect that his complex and mystical works can be unravelled and appreciated.

Blake could never have dreamed that his work *Jerusalem* would find a global audience by means of a musical adaptation. The poem was included in the patriotic anthology of verse *The Spirit of Man*, published in 1916. It was an attempt to boost morale in World War 1 and was edited by Robert Bridges, the Poet Laureate from 1913 to 1930. Bridges asked Sir Hubert Parry to set it to music for a public meeting of the 'Fight for Right' campaign in the Queen's Hall in London. Even King George V said that he preferred it to the national anthem, an opinion echoed by many people in the present day. It became a vital part of every *Last Night of the Proms* and is often used at major national and sporting events. A fitting tribute to a man whose work almost disappeared into oblivion.

Victor Hugo (1802–1885)

Victor-Marie Hugo was born on February 26th 1802 in Besançon, France and married Adèle Foucher (1803–1868) in 1822. He is renowned the world over for having written *Les Misérables* (1862), especially since its original musical adaptation, which had its premiere in Paris on September 24th 1980. His publishers agreed to pay him the huge sum of 300,000 Francs (around £3m today) for *Les Misérables*. In the story, Hugo gave Jean Valjean the prisoner number of 24601. Few people know that this derived from Hugo's belief that he was conceived on June 24th 1801. More than one hundred operas are based on Hugo's works and he named Berlioz and Liszt among his friends.

He also wrote *Notre Dame de Paris* (1831) known more commonly as *The Hunchback of Notre Dame* and this book both influenced and inspired Gaston Leroux's *Le Fantôme de l'Opéra* (1910). Hugo's literary output was considerable and he wrote a huge amount of poetry, plays, novels and essays during his career. What is less well known, especially outside France, is that he produced about 4,000 drawings.

When Napoleon III staged a coup d'état in December 1851, Hugo publicly announced that he was a traitor to France and was forced to flee to Belgium for a while. From Brussels, Hugo moved to live on Jersey, where he was introduced to Ouija boards and table tipping séances, hoping that he might be able to communicate with his daughter Léopoldine, who had drowned in a boating accident on the River Seine ten years earlier. He took part in many séances during 1852–1855, some led by the writer Delphine de Girardin (1804–1855) and some that he led himself. Using a planchette, he transcribed hundreds of automatic writings from other worldly spirits including Plato, Shakespeare, Galileo, Sir Walter Scott, and others. The conversations may be viewed as self-serving, wishful thinking, or as being summoned from the subconscious but it is important to remember that for any sincere participants in psychic exploration, they are real and immediate. Victor Hugo said of his voices that they were 'like his own mental powers multiplied by five'.

In 1855, Hugo was told to leave Jersey after he backed a Jersey newspaper that had printed criticism of Queen Victoria. He settled in Saint Peter Port, Guernsey where he was joined by his lover Juliette Drouet. In spite of a political amnesty in 1859, Hugo chose to remain in exile until Napoleon III's fall from power in 1870 and he was unable to attend his wife Adèle's funeral in 1868. During the fifteen years he lived on Guernsey, he wrote three acclaimed collections of poetry and the majority of *Les Misérables* which had taken him nearly twenty years to complete. He had made drawings of furniture and architecture since 1830 but during his time in the Channel Islands it ceased to be a hobby and he produced a huge amount of automatic drawing that he described as 'vagaries of the unknowing hand'. Some of the material was produced during séances without looking at the paper and frequently using the 'wrong' hand. Other drawings were made as a distraction from his serious writing and were given as gifts. He usually employed the same quill and ink for both activities and the drawings were predominantly small scale and rarely included colour. André Breton later declared that Hugo's automatist writings and artwork made him one of the forerunners of Surrealism.

He lived in Guernsey again during 1872–1873 before returning to France for the rest of his life.

He was not only revered as a literary figure, he was a statesman who shaped French democracy. Victor Hugo fought a lifelong battle against poverty and capital punishment. He campaigned for free education for all children, freedom of the press, universal suffrage, and an end to slavery in the United States.

He was incredibly eccentric and often sat naked at his desk until he had produced the amount of work he had set himself. He also had a huge appetite for sex, a lifestyle he was able to maintain until a few weeks before his death. He frequented brothels at all times of the day and sought women of all ages regardless of their background.

On his 80th birthday, he sat in his window and watched 600,000 people march past his house on Avenue d'Eylau for six hours in celebration. The following day, the street was renamed Avenue Victor-Hugo in his honour. He died of pneumonia on May 22nd 1885, at the age of 83 and the brothels of Paris closed down for a day of mourning. He was, in spite of his wishes for a pauper's funeral, given a state funeral by decree of President Jules Grévy. More than two million mourners joined the seven-hour procession to the burial in the Panthéon in Paris where he shares a crypt with Émile Zola and Alexandre Dumas. Hugo left his papers and drawings to the Bibliothèque nationale de Paris.

Allan Kardec (1804–1869)

Although automatic writing was not in itself the main reason for Kardec's inclusion in this book, it did lead to him becoming the founder of Spiritism, the French variation of Spiritualism. Spiritism, sometimes incorrectly termed Kardecism, stands by the principle that a series of compulsory reincarnations is necessary to achieve spiritual progress.

Allan Kardec was born Hypolyte Léon Denizard Rivail on October 3rd 1804 in Lyons, France. The son of a barrister, he studied at the Yverdon Institute in Switzerland from 1815 to 1822, qualified as a doctor of medicine and by 1850 had his own medical practice. In the intervening years, he worked as a teacher, translator, and writer and published twenty or more schoolbooks and educational texts. At that time, he stressed the importance of free thinking, religious tolerance, and the need for scientific knowledge. In view of his later life it is interesting to note a speech that Rivail made in 1834 in which he stated that 'the child who receives a good scientific education will no longer believe in souls from another world'.

He took an active interest in the activities of the Society of Magnetism, made investigations into hypnotism, clairvoyance, and trance and he became intrigued by the wave of Spiritualism that was spreading quickly across Europe. In 1855, Rivail attended several séances using a planchette and organised by a friend's two daughters before sitting with Celina Japhet (formerly Celina Bequet, a professional hypnotist). During the sessions with Celina, she received messages for Rivail telling him that he had been known as Allan and Kardec in past lives.

The automatic writings that Celina received whilst in trance explained the doctrine of compulsory reincarnation to Kardec and encouraged him to publish these beliefs in *Le Livre des Esprits* (The Spirits' Book) in 1856. The book described a new theory of human life and destiny and expanded Spiritualism beyond the tenet of survival after bodily death. It also prescribed a better understanding of healing, especially concerning epilepsy, schizophrenia, and multiple personality disorder, which was believed to be caused by the interference of past incarnations. The revised edition of 1857 became the recognised handbook of Spiritist philosophy in France and was printed in more than 25 editions and appeared in many different languages. It is still widely read, particularly in South America, Australia, and New Zealand. Kardec's books have had a huge influence in Brazil where there are thousands of associated temples and he has been commemorated on at least four issues of postage stamps. The success of *Le Livre des Esprits* prompted Kardec to publish *Le Livre des Mediums* (1861), *The Gospel According to Spiritism* (1864), *Heaven and Hell* (1865), and *Genesis - Miracles and*

Predictions According to Spiritism (1868). These five books are usually referred to as the 'Spiritist Codification', serve as the foundation to Spiritism, and have sold in their millions around the world.

During a séance, Kardec did not have the need for any sort of physical manifestation, neither did he seek investigative proof of any spirit communications. He had founded the monthly magazine *La Revue Spirite* in 1858, and later, the Society of Psychologic Studies. He took the opportunity they offered to deter the creation of the type of psychical research organisations that had been gaining ground in other countries. Unfortunately, this had the effect of holding back impartial research into psychical activities in France for many years. Both the magazine and the society steadfastly ignored several prominent mediums in France, especially if they disagreed with his approach to reincarnation. Kardec actively encouraged automatic writing, owing to the reduction of opposition arising from entrenched thinking.

Not long before his death in Paris on March 31st 1869, Kardec set up 'The Joint Stock Company for the Continuation of the Works of Allan Kardec'. The company was empowered to deal in the stock market and account for legacies and donations in order to maintain and perpetuate the Spiritist philosophy. Following his death, Spiritism waned in Europe and was replaced by Spiritualism and the fascination of physical phenomena.

In the U.K., the most prominent exponent of Kardec's work was Anna Blackwell. She translated his books into English and promoted their publication which led to the three-volume work *The Four Gospels* appearing in 1881.

Kardecism remains a potent force in Brazil with Kardecist healing centres operating alongside conventional hospitals.

Thomas Power James (c.1836–c.1892)

Whilst many people have sincere and genuine spiritual experiences, the nature of the psychic world leaves it vulnerable to fraud and malpractice. Even so, there are many cases where it is difficult to prove or disprove a case of automatic writing. From time to time, contact has been made with dead persons who were famous literary figures. These events are sometimes dismissed by critics, who automatically assume that the whole thing is preposterous. This judgement, made without any evidence or examination of a particular case is both unjust and unfair. Critics who approach a case from an impartial standpoint may well be surprised by the results. They may often come to the conclusion that a genuine and sincere medium combined with no evidence of fraudulent activity leaves them little room to condemn the communications under consideration. When Charles Dickens died on June 9th 1870, following years of poor health and two strokes, he left his fifteenth and possibly most ambitious novel unfinished. He had intended to publish *The Mystery of Edwin Drood* in twelve instalments but at the time of his death, only six, a total of 22 chapters, had been completed. Apart from providing a few hints to his friends, he left no notes giving any clues regarding the remaining six instalments nor any solution to the mystery. This left Dickens' army of readers in mid-story and without any answers regarding the novel's murder. Many writers have subsequently tried to complete the story but the most unusual was probably the attempt made by Thomas Power James, an itinerant printer from Vermont.

James was a mystery in his own right. He started or worked on newspapers in several towns but rarely stayed in a job for more than a year. He was a serial bigamist, married at least four but probably six or more women, and had a tendency to disappear. In 1863, he enlisted as an army musician during the American Civil War but was swiftly demoted when it was discovered that he could not play an instrument. He survived many ferocious battles before re-joining his wife Elizabeth in Nashua, New Hampshire. He then eloped with Martha, a boarder, to Massachusetts where he continued to work in the printing trade.

Shortly after moving to a boarding house in Brattleboro, Vermont he began working in the print shop of *The Vermont Record and Farmer* and his landlady invited him to join one of her circles and attend a séance. Initially sceptical about the idea, James was convinced about its validity when a table mysteriously moved towards him. He fell into a trance and wrote down things which seemed separate from himself and the communication was signed by persons who had died in Brattleboro before his arrival in town. The names could, of course, have been gleaned from his work and been lying in his subconscious. In a later spiritual gathering he received more writing, signed by Dickens, requesting that James be the instrument for the completion of the Edwin Drood story. James claimed that Dickens was so upset by his last work being unfinished that he was desperate to channel the missing manuscript through his own hand in the form of automatic writing. James worked either side of his ten-hour working day and his Edwin Drood continuation eventually filled 1,200 sheets of sermon paper. Before sinking into a deep trance (which could take from one to thirty minutes) he said that he was conscious of a Dickens like figure beside him with a grave face and with his head resting upon his hand. After he had recovered from the trance, he would find the room littered with sheets of paper containing Dickens' dictation. The handwriting did not match that of James but then it did not resemble Dickens' handwriting either. James' landlady, being a strong believer, even supplied him with free board and lodging until the work was finished. This was said to begin on November 15th 1872 followed by several intense and highly publicised sessions each week until its completion and publication in October 1873 under the titles *Part Second of the Mystery of Edwin Drood* (also as *The Mystery of Edwin Drood, Complete*). It received a review by *The New York Times* and other newspapers which gave support to a successful marketing campaign. The book soon became a bestseller and James was offered contracts to write more books but he refused them, stating that Dickens had chosen him to complete his last work and that he would not produce any further books. At the time, people were sceptical about the affair but the opinion in Brattleboro was that James had neither the power nor the education to do the work unaided.

After the book's completion, he started producing his spiritualist magazine *The Summerland Messenger* in September 1873. He used the magazine to serialise the next two books he claimed to have received from Dickens. They were *The Life and Adventures of Bockley Whickleheap*, and *The Story of Humpback's Pilgrimage*. The only surviving copy of *The Summerland Messenger* is Volume 2 Number 4 which was the 10th edition and contains the second chapter of *Bockley Whickleheap*. In spite of a scandal, James was still able to become the co-editor and publisher of *The Windham County Reformer* in 1878 which was the forerunner of *The Brattleboro Reformer*. In the 1880s, he moved to Maine with his family and started *The Sanford Herald* in 1884. This paper is the last known publication we have for James. Following a successful beginning, he urged subscribers and advertisers to pay for the second year in advance but absconded back to Massachusetts, where he became the editor of *The Waltham Times* in October 1885. James was known to be working as a reporter in Boston in the 1890s but then disappeared from history.

In spite of the book's success in the United States, James' ending to *Edwin Drood* was not generally accepted by the U.K. aficionados of Dickens' works. There had been previous attempts to finish the book but James' rendering was the most unusual. And though Dickens had been sceptical and suspicious of spiritualists during his lifetime, he had also experienced psychic occurrences for which he could give no rational explanation.

Arthur Conan Doyle wrote an essay titled *The Alleged Posthumous Writings of Great Authors* on the subject which appeared in *The Bookman* (December 1927 [U.S.]) and in *The Fortnightly Review* (December 1927 [U.S.]. Conan Doyle endorsed and commended the work, stating that it resembled Dickens' style. He wrote 'It seems to me to be like Dickens — but Dickens gone flat. The fizz, the sparkle, the spontaneity of it is gone. But the trick of thought and of manner remains. If it be indeed a parody it has the rare merit among parodies of never accentuating or exaggerating the peculiarities of the original'. It caused a literary sensation at the time but since then, Dickensian scholars have dismissed the work of Thomas Power James as being frivolous and illiterate. Yet James had received scant education, regularly attended the Episcopalian church, was a model citizen, and knew little about Spiritualism. It seems unlikely that anyone like James would invest so much of his time and effort in a deliberate literary fraud. In recent years, interest in TP James has gathered momentum and there is an annual writing contest held in Brattleboro to commemorate James' part in the town's history.

William Stainton Moses (1839–1892)

William Stainton Moses was born on November 5th 1839 in Donington, Lincoln, England and was ordained as a Church of England priest in 1870. He became interested in Spiritualism and séances in spite of his initial scepticism. He attended his first séance in April 1872 with Lottie Fowler, receiving information from a deceased friend. This converted him to Spiritualism and just a few months later, he claimed to experience levitation.

He published *Psychography – A Treatise on One of the Objective Forms of Psychic or Spiritual Phenomena* (1878), in which he coins the word psychography, promulgating the idea of communicating with the dead using automatic writing.

His automatic writings may be found in his books *Spirit Identity* (1879) and *Spirit Teachings* (1883), sometimes called the 'Bible of Spiritualism'. He was occasionally sceptical of his writings but they eventually led him away from the Anglican Church and towards Spiritualism. In 1884, Moses was a founding member and the first president of the London Spiritualist Alliance, later to become the College of Psychic Studies. He believed that his messages were coming from higher spirits and were intended for the benefit of humanity. The messages were delivered by 'Imperator', who was supposedly the chief of a band of 49 spirits from the 'seventh sphere', and other spirits such as 'Rector' and 'Mentor'. Moses handwriting was markedly different depending on the communicator.

He was editor of the magazine *LIGHT* (1881), the oldest psychic journal still in publication. In 1882, along with Frederic William Myers, he helped found the Society for Psychical Research. Myers was strongly impressed by Moses' abilities and was convinced of his honesty but never understood him. Moses resigned from the SPR in 1886 following their investigation of the medium William Eglinton.

His earlier support for the spirit photography of the disgraced Édouard Isidore Buguet threw doubts on his integrity and his séances, performed in a dark room with close friends, produced doubtful phenomena. He never allowed himself to be tested and psychical researchers considered him to have created the phenomena by his own hands in spite of his reputation for complete integrity.

When he died on September 5th 1892 in Bedford, Stainton Moses bequeathed his extensive library to the college and 23 of his 24 notebooks of automatic or 'directed' writings are stored in the College of Psychic Studies archives in South Kensington, London.

Arthur Conan Doyle (1859–1930)

Arthur Conan Doyle, the Scottish writer and creator of the Sherlock Holmes stories, was born on May 22nd 1859 in Edinburgh.

Automatic writing became very popular during the Victorian age of Spiritualism, which had been in the doldrums for decades. Later, the huge loss of life in World War One had left innumerable families mourning the death of their loved ones and people attended séances in large numbers hoping to receive messages from beyond the grave. Unfortunately, their grief was making them susceptible to charlatans and many people set themselves up as mediums solely to benefit from the demand.

Conan Doyle was a great supporter of Spiritualism and donated large amounts of money to the cause. He published the following as a supplementary document in *The New Revelation* (1918).

'Automatic Writing'

This form of mediumship gives the very highest results, and yet in its very nature is liable to self-deception. Are we using our own hand or is an outside power directing it? It is only by the information received that we can tell, and even then we have to make broad allowance for the action of our own subconscious knowledge. It is worthwhile perhaps to quote what appears to me to be a thoroughly critic-proof case, so that the inquirer may see how strong the evidence is that these messages are not self-evolved. This case is quoted in Mr. Arthur Hill's recent book *Man Is a Spirit* (Cassell 1918) and is contributed by a gentleman who takes the name of Captain James Burton. He is, I understand, the same medium (amateur) through whose communications the position of the buried ruins at Glastonbury have recently been located. 'A week after my father's funeral I was writing a business letter, when something seemed to intervene between my hand and the motor centres of my brain, and the hand wrote at an amazing rate a letter, signed with my father's signature and purporting to come from him. I was upset, and my right side and arm became cold and numb. For a year after this letters came frequently, and always at unexpected times. I never knew what they contained until I examined them with a magnifying glass: they were microscopic. And they contained a vast amount of matter with which it was impossible for me to be acquainted.' ... 'Unknown to me, my mother, who was staying some sixty miles away, lost her pet dog, which my father had given her. The same night I had a letter from him condoling with her, and stating that the dog was now with him. All things which love us and are necessary to our happiness in the world are with us here.'

A most sacred secret, known to no one but my father and mother, concerning a matter which occurred years before I was born, was afterwards told me in the script, with the comment: 'Tell your mother this, and she will know that it is I, your father, who am writing.' My mother had been unable to accept the possibility up to now but when I told her this, she collapsed and fainted. From that moment the letters became her greatest comfort, for they were lovers during the forty years of their married life, and his death almost broke her heart.

'As for myself, I am as convinced that my father, in his original personality, still exists as if he were still in his study with the door shut. He is no more dead than he would be were he living in America.'

'I have compared the diction and vocabulary of these letters with those employed in my own writing — I am not unknown as a magazine contributor — and I find no points of similarity between the two.' There is much further evidence in this case for which I refer the reader to the book itself.

Arthur Conan Doyle died on July 7th 1930 in Crowborough, Sussex. He was buried at the nearby All Saints Church, Minstead. His wife, now Lady Jean Conan Doyle, was buried at the same place in 1940.

Jean Elizabeth Leckie (1874–1940)

Conan Doyle's second wife, Jean Elizabeth (Leckie) was born in Kidbrook, Kent on March 14th 1874 and, like her husband, was also an ardent spiritualist. She produced a substantial amount of automatic writing without entering a state of trance. In the company of just a few people and with pen and paper to hand, she would write a cross on the paper and Arthur would offer a suitable prayer. Within a short time, she would get the impetus to start writing although not be conscious of the words that appeared on the paper. Her spirit guide was named 'Pheneas' who predicted global disasters on a regular basis. The Conan Doyles even received 'advice' on when to travel or move house although this did occasionally concur with Jean's own personal wishes. In spite of the messages being received through Jean, it was Arthur's name that appeared on the title page when he published *Pheneas Speaks* (1927).

In 1920, Conan Doyle met the famed escapologist and illusionist Harry Houdini for the first time. It was an unlikely friendship, made by them both having a strong interest in Spiritualism. Houdini had a strong desire to communicate with his deceased mother but was held back by his intimate knowledge of what could be theatrically engineered. Before becoming an escapologist, he and his wife Bess would create 'séances' as part of their vaudeville act. Houdini later fronted a campaign to expose the charlatans and frauds that he deemed 'human leeches'.

In an Atlantic City hotel room in 1922, the Doyles met Houdini in an attempt to communicate with his mother. Jean produced fifteen pages of automatic writing, seemingly to have originated from the dead woman, and they appeared to have an emotional effect on Houdini. However, Houdini stated publicly afterwards that he did not believe that the message from beyond the grave was genuine, not least because the quality of the writing was nothing like his mother's poor command of English. The letter began with a cross, an inappropriate symbol because the lady was Jewish and had been married to a rabbi. In addition, the letter referred to Houdini as 'Harry' but having been born Erik Weisz, his mother had only ever used his real name. When Houdini's mission to unmask fraudulent spiritualist mediums named people that Conan Doyle respected as being genuine, their friendship broke down and the two men had not become reconciled before Houdini died from a ruptured appendix in 1926. He had desperately wanted to believe that Spiritualism was genuine but his own investigations had convinced him that it wasn't.

Jean Elizabeth Conan Doyle died in London on June 27th 1940.

Hélène Smith (1861–1929)

One of the most celebrated automatic writers was the Swiss medium Hélène Smith. Born Catherine Elise Müller in Martigny on December 9th 1861, she discovered Spiritualism in 1891 and within a year was displaying mediumistic abilities and communicating with Victor Hugo. She held countless séances for friends and followers, mostly between 1894 and 1901, but was never paid for her mediumship. She declared that she had past lives as the Hindu Princess Simandini and Marie Antoinette and produced automatic writing in multiple languages. Smith also claimed to have received messages in the languages of Uranus and Mars which she translated into her native language (French) and this popularised automatic writing. Her main communicators were 'Léopold', a reincarnation of Joseph Balsamo or the Count de Cagliostro (Marie Antoinette's lover) and 'Esenale', a reincarnation of Alexis Mirbel, the deceased son of one of her sitters.

In Geneva, she became friends with Théodore Flournoy, Professor of Psychology at the University of Geneva. First published in 1899, his book about her life *Des Indes à la Planete Mars* (From India to the Planet Mars) made her famous. The book detailed her experiences as being in romantic cycles, these being the Martian, Ultramartian, Hindu, Oriental, and royal cycles. Hélène's trances often took her to Mars where she described the landscape and its people. She also appeared to speak and write the Martian language.

Flournoy made a study of Smith's work, concluding that the cycles were just a product of a childish imagination and 'romances of the subliminal imagination'. Flournay also stated that her 'Martian' alphabet was a product of her subconscious although other researchers disagreed and stated that the alphabet was extra-terrestrial.

When she became estranged from Flournoy, a wealthy American spiritualist from Connecticut, Mrs Ellen Jackson, offered her a salary in order that she could concentrate on Christian Spiritualism and this enabled her to create religious paintings of Christ.

Smith was popular with the Surrealists who dubbed her 'the Muse of Automatic Writing'. They considered her to be proof of the power of the surreal, and symbolic of the movement's aims. Following her death in Geneva on June 10th 1929, the Geneva Art Museum exhibited a retrospective of her work.

WB Yeats (1865–1939) & Georgie Hyde-Lees (1892–1968)

Another writer who was closely involved with automatic writing was the Irish poet and dramatist William Butler Yeats. He was born on June 13th 1865 in Sandymount, Ireland. On October 20th 1917, he married Georgie Hyde-Lees, having first met her at the British Museum when she was seventeen. Georgie was born on October 16th 1892 in Fleet, Hampshire. During their unsuccessful honeymoon, he became fascinated by her ability to produce automatic writing although they referred to it as 'the automatic script'. Their early years together were a period of extensive experimentation in the subject. This helped to stabilise their relationship which was being undermined by his continued pursuit of Maud Gonne and her daughter Iseult following their rejection of his marriage proposals. In the first three years of his marriage to Georgie, she received 4,000 pages of handwritten automatic writing during 450 sessions. Possibly by accident but more likely by design, the writings encouraged Yeats to cease his interest in the other women, suggested he improve his diet, and instructed on the days in the month when Georgie was most likely to conceive. They even advised on how Yeats could make sex more enjoyable, particularly for Georgie. Even if the rest of her writings were genuine, it seems that she had found her own way of saving the marriage and making it more tolerable for herself.

Yeats disliked the name Georgie and always referred to her as George. She would go into a trance and call up various spirit guides which they called 'instructors'. She received an intricate esoteric system of history and philosophy from them which Yeats revealed in *A Vision* (1925). Although Georgie had provided most of the content of the book, it was Yeats who was credited as the author. Yeats published a revised edition of the book in 1937 and offered to dedicate it to Georgie. It read 'To my wife, who created this system which bores her, who made possible these pages which she will never read…' Unsurprisingly, she rejected it. Soon after Yeats' death in Menton, France on January 28th 1939, she edited *A Vision* for an immediate new edition and continued to edit the work collected in later editions of Yeats' poems. Georgie outlived her husband by nearly 30 years and died on August 23rd 1968 in Rathmines, Dublin. Decades passed before it was recognised that Georgie had provided much of the material for Yeats' poetry. In 1988, the renowned Yeats scholar Margaret Mills Harper wrote 'We are having to take an extraordinary fact into far more serious consideration than we have before. Much of the literary output of one of our century's major poets from the year of his marriage on was directly influenced by a unique imaginative partnership with a highly creative woman.'

Rudyard Kipling (1865–1936)

Joseph Rudyard Kipling was born in Malabar Hill, Bombay (Mumbai) on December 30th 1865. His parents spent many years in India where their father, John Lockwood Kipling (1837–1911), worked as an artist and illustrator. In 1870, the family made a brief visit to England and Alice and her brother Rudyard were heartlessly abandoned at a boarding home in Southsea, England when their parents went back to India. They suffered a woeful experience at the hands of a violent governess named Mrs Sarah Holloway and her bully-boy son who terrified them with Old Testament threats of hellfire and damnation if they stepped out of line. After his hideous experience in Southsea, he was sent to the United Services College at Westward Ho! in Devon in 1878. Aged just thirteen, he was subjected to yet more boarding school bullying in the early years but settled down and completed four years there before returning to India where he took up a position as a journalist with *The Civil and Military Gazette* in Lahore. He encountered spiritualists in India whilst working as a journalist and displayed a strong interest in the occult throughout his life. He may also have been influenced by his father who attended a séance with Madame Blavatsky during her visit to Simla in 1880. Afterwards, he declared that she was 'one of the most interesting and unscrupulous impostors' he had ever met. He wrote every form of content for the *Gazette*, including dozens of short stories, but by 1889 he had wider horizons and returned to Britain via the Far East and the United States before his arrival in London. With the help of his father his writings appeared in many magazines. The sudden exposure made him a star almost overnight at the age of 22. The 1890s saw Kipling at the height of his popularity. In December 1891, he returned to London for a funeral and met and proposed to Caroline Starr Balestier. They were married on January 18th 1892 and she was a great support to him throughout his life. They went to live in Dummerston, Vermont where their three children were born and where he wrote *The Jungle Books* (1893-94). The political situation and their domestic scene became unstable and they returned to Britain, first to Torquay in Devon and then Ringwood in Hampshire. Their final home was 'Batemans', a country house not far from Burwash in Sussex.

He tried to persuade Alice to stay away from spirit writing but she considered it too important to give up and suffered a breakdown. Alice's persistent mental illness that began in 1898 was the overriding factor in his resistance to Spiritualism.

Rudyard Kipling was appalled at the number of bogus spiritualists that set themselves up as mediums in the wake of World War 1. He published a poem in 1918 warning distressed family members who had lost a loved one during the war not to part with their money in the hope of receiving a message of comfort from the deceased. Although not in keeping with the exact theme of this book, I considered it worthy of inclusion here nonetheless. One would imagine that Alice's mental state was uppermost in Kipling's mind at the time of writing *En-Dor*.

En-Dor
'Behold there is a woman that hath a familiar spirit at En-Dor.'
I Samuel xxviii 7.

THE ROAD to En-dor is easy to tread
For Mother or yearning Wife.
There, it is sure, we shall meet our Dead
As they were even in life.
Earth has not dreamed of the blessing in store
For desolate hearts on the road to En-dor.

Whispers shall comfort us out of the dark—
Hands—ah God!—that we knew!
Visions and voices — look and hark!—
Shall prove that the tale is true,
An that those who have passed to the further shore
May' be hailed — at a price — on the road to En-dor.

But they are so deep in their new eclipse
Nothing they say can reach,
Unless it be uttered by alien lips
And framed in a stranger's speech.
The son must send word to the mother that bore,
'Through an hireling's mouth. 'Tis the rule of En-dor.

And not for nothing these gifts are shown
By such as delight our dead.
They must twitch and stiffen and slaver and groan
Ere the eyes are set in the head,
And the voice from the belly begins. Therefore,
We pay them a wage where they ply at En-dor.
Even so, we have need of faith
And patience to follow the clue.
Often, at first, what the dear one saith
Is babble, or jest, or untrue.
152

(Lying spirits perplex us sore
Till our loves—and their lives—are well-known at En-dor). .
Oh the road to En-dor is the oldest road
And the craziest road of all!
Straight it runs to the Witch's abode,
As it did in the days of Saul,
And nothing has changed of the sorrow in store
For such as go down on the road to En-dor!

The year after *En-dor* appeared, Rudyard renounced any connection with Spiritualism. This seems to have more to do with the protection of both his sister and his perceived reputation than any firm rejection of the subject. An examination of his autobiography *Something of Myself: for my friends known and unknown* (1937) reveals that some of his work appears to be inspired by automatic writing. The book, edited and published by his wife after his death, skips over much of his personal life and tends to concentrate on his work. He makes fourteen mentions of his 'daemon', a name he bestowed on a spirit that was instrumental in the writing that he produced. Some of the references were unequivocal regarding their association with automatic writing.

(a) 'My pen took charge and I, greatly admiring, watched it write for me far into the nights.'

(b) 'After blocking out the main idea in my head, the pen took charge, and I watched it begin to write stories about Mowgli and animals, which later grew into the *Jungle Books.'*

(c) 'My Daemon was with me in the *Jungle Books*, *Kim*, and both Puck books, and good care I took to walk delicately, lest he should withdraw.'

(d) 'When your Daemon is in charge, do not try to think consciously. Drift, wait, and obey.'

Kipling was asked for his opinion on Spiritualism and whether it had any foundation in fact. He replied 'There is, I know. Have nothing to do with it.' One must presume that his response was coloured by thoughts of his sister's mental illness at the time.

In January 1936, he had surgery for an intestinal haemorrhage but died at the Middlesex Hospital, London on January 18th 1936. He was cremated and his ashes lie in Westminster Abbey, next to the graves of Thomas Hardy and Charles Dickens. News of his death had been printed by mistake some years earlier. He wrote to the offending magazine saying 'I've just read that I am dead. Don't forget to delete me from your list of subscribers'. Lovely.

Hester Dowden (1868–1949)

Hester Meredith Dowden was born on May 3rd 1868 in Dublin, Ireland and became one of the most famous spiritualist mediums of the twentieth century. A friend and colleague of Geraldine Cummins, Hester Dowden used both her maiden name and her married name, Travers-Smith. She had married the eminent Dublin physician Richard Travers-Smith on February 4th 1896 to escape her stepmother. After he had he confessed to an affair with a patient in 1915, Hester moved to London. She was granted a divorce in November 1922 and reverted to her maiden name by deed poll. She had at least five spirit guides helping her with her automatic writing and she is perhaps most notable for having claimed to have contacted the spirit of Oscar Wilde (1854–1900) more than twenty years after he died. The messages arrived partly by means of automatic writing and partly by the use of a planchette or Ouija board. When she published *Psychic Messages from Oscar Wilde* (1923), there was a spat in *The Psychic Review* between Charles W Soal and Arthur Conan Doyle. Soal, who occasionally helped Hester with the work, said that she was the true author of the text even if she was not aware of the fact whereas Conan Doyle was adamant that the author was obviously Oscar Wilde. In the messages, Wilde revealed that he adored women and that he was not a homosexual. At first glance, this seems to undermine the legitimacy of Hester's writings until one realises that his statement about his sexuality is basically correct for he was quite clearly bisexual. He married Constance Lloyd in 1884 and retained a great fondness for his childhood sweetheart, Florence Balcombe, who later married Bram Stoker. Another point of view, of course, is that Hester was a great admirer of Wilde and could not accept him as being anything other than heterosexual. Strangely, Wilde said that he could not read on the other side and was only able to do so through the eyes of the living, giving him access to the works of George Bernard Shaw, John Galsworthy, Thomas Hardy, and James Joyce. Hester said that Wilde had told her 'that being dead was as boring as being married or having dinner with a schoolmaster'. Hester even received a three act play that Wilde was supposed to have written in the spirit world entitled *The Extraordinary Play* although this was later retitled *Is it a Forgery?* Only one copy of the script is known to exist and it is stored at The Clark Library at UCLA in Los Angeles. It is interesting to note that Hester was probably the model for the medium in WB Yeats's play *The Words upon the Window Pane* (1930).

Hester Dowden only published two books in her own name, the other one being her autobiography *Voices from the Void* (1919). In this, she gives an account of her contact with the spirit of Sir Hugh Lane (1875-1915), the

Irish art dealer and collector who had perished on May 7th 1915 when the RMS Lusitania had been sunk by a German U-Boat off the west coast of Cork, Ireland. He had established Dublin's Municipal Gallery of Modern Art but when it opened in January 1908, Dublin Corporation refused to meet the long-term running costs. In despair, Lane bequeathed his pictures to the National Gallery in London but just before his death, he attached a codicil to his will that left the collection to Ireland. The codicil was not witnessed leading to a long-term dispute over ownership although an equitable agreement was eventually reached. Lane apparently contacted Hester to confirm his wish for the paintings to remain in Dublin. Although news of Lane's death had appeared in the newspapers on the day of the spirit message, Hester stated that she had not read the papers that day.

Hester was consulted at least twice on the provenance of Shakespeare's plays. Alfred Dodd wanted to prove that Francis Bacon was the true author of the works but Percy Allen wanted to prove that they were penned by Edward de Vere, Earl of Oxford. When asked, the spirits confirmed the assertion on both occasions and also provided previously unknown details of Shakespeare's life. Hester also published 'Shakespearian' sonnets and parts of plays but this influence may have stemmed from her father, Professor Edward Dowden (1843-1913), who was a renowned expert on Shakespeare and wrote many books on the subject.

In 1941, Hester claimed to have received messages from an ancient Greek philosopher 'Johannes' (one of her spirit guides) that made observations about the national leaders during World War 2. Hitler, Stalin, Churchill, and Roosevelt all fell under the spotlight. 'Johannes' said that Hitler was not evil but 'a man whose stars threw him into the world with vast disadvantages, with overwhelming ambition sweltering in his soul, and with an infinite capacity for receiving influences and suggestions from our side.' Stalin was seen as being 'crafty and careful'. Churchill she said 'can be hot-headed, full of zeal and enthusiasm, and, at the same time, never lose his balance in the least'. Roosevelt was described as an 'intricate personality' who is 'affectionate, and has a genuine love for the human race. He is not fond of adventure, as Churchill is, but he would not shirk risks if he felt they might set things in the right direction'.

Hester Dowden died on February 16th 1949 after suffering a stroke and falling into an electric fire at her home in London. Her cremated remains were buried at Golders Green. In her lifetime, Hester claimed to have given more than 40,000 sittings, including the former Queen Victoria Eugenia of Spain.

Alice Fleming (1868–1948)

Alice began automatic writing in India and was one of the principal mediums in the cases of 'cross correspondence'. She was born Alice Macdonald Kipling in Fulham, London on June 11th 1868, the younger sister of author Rudyard Kipling. She was given the nickname 'Trix' by her family when she was young because she was 'a tricksy little baby'.

Her mother (also named Alice MacDonald Kipling) along with her sisters, experimented with 'table turning' and encouraged the children's interest in the occult. As a result, Alice inherited psychic capabilities from her mother and her aunts and from a young age she was able to see ghosts.

Their parents spent many years in India where their father, John Lockwood Kipling (1837–1911), worked as an artist and illustrator in Bombay (Mumbai) and Lahore (part of India until 1947). In 1970, the family made a brief visit to England and Alice and her brother Rudyard were heartlessly abandoned at a boarding home 'for the children of Indian Army officers' in Southsea, England whilst their parents went back to India for five years. They were given a private education but suffered a woeful experience at the hands of a monstrous and violent governess named Mrs Sarah Holloway who terrified them with Old Testament threats of hellfire and damnation if they stepped out of line. Around 1884, at the age of sixteen, Alice returned to India and settled with her family in Lahore where her father was the principal of the Mayo School of Arts and Crafts. In that year, she and Rudyard published a book of poetry entitled *Echoes* (1884). She later married John Murchison Fleming (1858–1942), a British army officer ten years her senior who worked for the Survey of India until his retirement in 1911. Her parents probably disapproved of the marriage because the wedding took place on her 21st birthday on June 11th 1889 at Simla in Bengal. The marriage was not a success for Alice and she became unhappy, lonely, and isolated from her family.

Life took a turn for the better when she published her first novel *The Heart of a Maid* (1890) in the name of Beatrice Grange at the age of 22. Later editions printed the author's name as Beatrice Kipling. It seemed profoundly autobiographical, describing the fear of intimacy about to be endured following marriage. A second novel followed entitled *A Pinchbeck Goddess* (1897) which also appeared to echo her own apprehension at revealing too much of herself when her name appeared on the cover as 'Mrs JM Fleming'. Her unhappy marriage restricted the flow of her writing and she never completed a third novel.

She found solace in crystal gazing and the automatic writing that began in 1893 when she was 25. She frequently received it in the form of poetry or as letters for her friends from their deceased family members.

In 1898, Alice became ill with depression for a long period of time but her husband refused to allow her any treatment by psychologists. She returned to England in 1902 to recuperate but it was to be the first of the mental health issues which would punctuate her life. Even so, she was a prolific writer though she was considerably outshined by her brother. She wrote poetry and fiction throughout her life, both with her family and independently. Many of her numerous stories and articles, especially about Anglo Indian life, were published in magazines in Britain and India. In 1902, she published a book of poetry *Hand in Hand: Verses by a Mother and Daughter* with her mother Alice Kipling.

She returned to India and became involved in the strange phenomenon known as 'cross correspondence' whereby several individuals receive automatic writings and each one only contains a part of a complete message. The six or seven women concerned were apparently unknown to each other and lived many miles apart.

Shortly after reading *Human Personality and Its Survival of Bodily Death* by Frederic WH Myers (1843–1901), she received a stream of spirit messages from Myers via automatic writing, the first of which arrived on September 19th 1903. He asked her to forward the messages to the British Society of Psychical Research (BSPR) and she complied with the request by writing to the BSPR secretary Alice Johnson. Alice Fleming transcribed another message from Myers on January 17th 1904 that included the reference 'I Cor. xvi 13'. More than 4,000 miles away in England, Margaret Verrall received the same message on the same day via automatic writing. The King James Version of the bible gives 'I Cor. xvi 13' as 'Watch ye, stand fast in the faith, quit you like men, be strong'. This passage from the bible is inscribed in Greek 'ΣΤΗΚΕΤΕ ΕΝ ΤΗ ΠΙΣΤΕΙ ΑΝΔΡΙΖΣΘΕ' over the main entrance of Selwyn College, Cambridge. Myers had studied at Trinity College a short distance away and was said to have frequently passed under the gateway. Margaret Verrall lived and died at 5 Selwyn Gardens, barely a hundred yards from Selwyn College and the inscription would probably have been known to her too but Alice Fleming appears to have little or no familiarity with Cambridge.

Alice also transcribed automatic writings from the psychologist Edmund Gurney (1847–1888) who had befriended Myers at Trinity and the poet Roden Noel (1834–1894), both of whom were unknown to her. She was instructed by Noel to ask 'AW' about the significance of May 26th 1894 and if he did not know, that he should ask 'Nora'. The message had no meaning for Alice but she did send it on to the BSPR in London. They realised that

'AW' referred to Margaret Verrall's husband Dr Arthur Woollgar Verrall (1851–1912) and that Nora was Dr Eleanor (Nora) Sidgwick (1845–1936). May 26th 1894 was the day that Roden Noel died in Mainz railway station, Germany. The BSPR took her messages extremely seriously and viewed her as one of the most notable psychics of the period and she became one of the few respected mediums of her era. Nowadays, her automatic writing is likely to be attributed as stemming from her subconscious owing to her intense psychological suffering but whatever the origin, her writings will forever remain a source of interest and fascination.

Alice continued to pursue her interest in automatic writing until 1910, when she and John Fleming moved from India to Edinburgh. Shortly after their arrival, Alice received news that her mother had passed away and she suffered a nervous breakdown. Her mental illness worsened when her father died three months later and she was beset with problems for the next ten years. In an attempt to stabilise her health, she was moved from place to place at regular intervals. John Fleming frequently clashed with her family regarding the treatment of her illness, which they attributed to her psychic interests. After years of living apart, Alice returned to Scotland in 1932 to live with her husband in a large house in Edinburgh. She rebuilt her life, the fun returned to it and she was always seen wearing fine clothes. After the death of her brother Rudyard in 1936, she helped found The Kipling Society and wrote articles for *The Kipling Journal*. Also, she assisted in the restoration of Rudyard's reputation, which had become tainted after World War 1 when his writings saw him viewed as a jingoistic imperialist. In 1943, she took over the lease of a shop in Edinburgh. 'Gifts and Gratitude' raised money for army charities. Alice was also a regular visitor to Edinburgh Zoo and would talk to the elephants in Hindustani. Remarkably, she became a member of the Edinburgh Psychic College (founded 1932) which still exists at 2 Melville Street, just a short walk from The Sir Arthur Conan Doyle Centre. Alice also wrote articles for *The Psychic Press* although she used the pseudonym 'Mrs Holland' to satisfy the wishes of the family, who were opposed to her being publicly involved with the occult. She lived in Edinburgh for the rest of her life and died on October 25th 1948 at her home at 6 West Coates, Edinburgh. The house is now an attractive hotel, making it possible for interested parties to visit her home.

Emily Grant Hutchings (1870–1960)

Emily Grant Hutchings had sat with Pearl Curran when Patience Worth surfaced in 1913 and by 1916 she claimed to have received three manuscripts from Samuel Clemens (Mark Twain). She was born Emily Schmidt to German parents in Hannibal, Missouri on January 30th 1870. Emily attended school in Hannibal before going to Altenburg in Germany, the birthplace of her father Carl Herman Schmidt, to attend a famous girls' school for a year, the Karolinum Hohere Tochtere Schule. On returning to the United States, she entered Columbia State University where she obtained a degree in Letters. She taught Latin, Greek, and German at Hannibal High School for two years and then went to St Louis to work as a feature writer for the *St Louis Republic* during 1896–1897. During a journey to Memphis, she met Charles Edwin Hutchings. He had seen her article on Mark Twain in *McClure's Magazine* and before their return to St Louis, they found that they had mutual interests. She married Hutchings, a newspaper man from Clarinda, Iowa, in 1897.

Emily and Edwin first met Mark Twain, a native of Hannibal, when he addressed the St Louis Art Students' Association on June 7th 1902. She was fascinated by his writing and they exchanged correspondence over the next year or so with Twain offering words of advice and encouragement.

Mark Twain died on April 21st 1910. In 1916, Emily Hutchings claimed that Twain dictated several manuscripts to her via the medium Lola Viola Hays using a Ouija board. During one session, with Emily in attendance, Lola received the words 'Samuel L. Clemens, lazy Sam. Well, why don't some of you say something? Say, folks, don't knock my memoirs too hard. They were written when Mark Twain was dead to all sense of decency. When brains are soft, the method should be anaesthesia.' Over a period of two years, Emily received two short stories, *Up the Furrow to Fortune* and *A Daughter of Mars*, and a 50,000-word manuscript that they would publish the following year. Lola was the passive recipient whose hands guided the Ouija board and when she asked Twain why he had waited six years to give his new material to the world, he had responded that he would transmit the stories through her if she could find the right person to sit with her at the Ouija board. In the Introduction to the book *Jap Herron*, Emily said that Twain had been waiting for someone to come along with whom he could form a connection and dictate his work. She thinks he chose her because she was also from Hannibal, Missouri. During an early session, Twain told Emily and Lola that they could edit minor errors, but not to attempt to correct his grammar. He also told them that he knew what he wanted to say. 'And, dear ladies, when I say d-a-m-n, please don't write d-a-r-n. Don't try to smooth it out. This is not a smooth story.' The two ladies were amused that Twain should fear the blue pencil at their hands. When the work was nearing completion, Twain would say that he or the ladies were tired, so it would be time to stop for a rest. He also warned them on a few occasions to be wary of other spirits interrupting the process with their own ideas. Emily's husband also sat in on the proceedings. He added ten punctuation marks to the Ouija board to help speed up the process whereupon Twain remarked that 'Edwin did a pretty piece of work'.

In 1917, *Jap Herron: A Novel Written from the Ouija Board* was published in New York. The book rose to fame when The New York Times ran this less than flattering review of it on September 9th 1917.

'The Ouija board seems to have come to stay as a competitor of the typewriter in the production of fiction. For this is the third novel in the last few months that has claimed the authorship of some dead and gone being who, unwilling to give up human activities, has appeared to find in the Ouija board a material means of expression. This last story is unequivocal in its claim of origin. For those who are responsible for it appear to be convinced beyond doubt that no less a spirit than that of Mark Twain guided their hands as the story was spelled out on the board. Emily Grant Hutchings and Lola V. Hays are the sponsors of the tale. Mrs. Hays being the passive recipient whose hands upon the pointer were especially necessary. St Louis is the scene of the exploit, as it is also of the literary labors of that Ouija board that writes the 'Patience Worth' stories. Emily Grant Hutchings, who writes the introductory account of how it all happened, is from Hannibal, Missouri, the home of Mark Twain's boyhood, and in her the alleged spirit of the author seems to have put much confidence. Her long description of how the story was written and of the many conversations they had with Mark Twain through the Ouija board contains many quotations of his remarks that sometimes have a reminiscent flavor of the humorist's characteristic conversation.'

Owing to the popularity of Ouija boards at the time, many Americans purchased the book regardless of the review and accepted Hutchings' claims at face value. Clara Clemens, Twain's daughter, and Harper and Brothers, the publishing company that owned the sole rights to the books of Mark Twain, filed a lawsuit in the Supreme Court. Clemens and her publishers were unable to prove that the book was not written by the ghost of Twain but Emily Hutchings was required to either admit that the book was a fraud or surrender all profits to the Mark Twain estate and Harper & Brothers. Emily never retracted her claims but the case never went to trial as she and her publisher Mitchell Kennerley agreed to halt publication. The case attracted huge attention from the newspapers of the time and they followed the story for several weeks. Most copies of *Jap Herron* were destroyed making it a rarity but it can be found online where it can be read without charge.

Emily's writing output was prodigious and she contributed large amounts of poetry and fiction in addition to the hundreds of features she wrote for newspapers and magazines. She was a relentless researcher and would forage endlessly for material until she found what she was looking for. Some research could lie dormant in her mind for as long as two years or more when suddenly without warning it would present itself fully formed to be written down without making any changes. Her work was usually sent to the publishers just as first written, attributing this to the fact that all of her good work is the result of 'subconscious cerebration' a phrase that she had derived from one of Twain's letters. She often discovered notes she did not recall as her own except for her initials at the end.

She had held the position of librarian and lecturer at the St Louis School of Fine Arts and during the World's Fair in St Louis in 1904, this enabled her appointment to the staff of the General Press Bureau, writing a story a day for 24 weeks and they were printed all over the world.

The manner in which she obtained the material for *The Exile*, one of her stories, is fairly typical of her methods. One day, whilst washing the dishes, she was distracted by the call of 'rags, bottles, and old iron!' in the alley behind the house. She stopped her housework, gathered a pencil and notepad, and wrote as fast as she could. After she had finished, Emily returned to the dishes but had no definite impression of how the story had been arranged.

Emily Rosalie Schmidt Grant Hutchings died in St Louis, Missouri on January 18th 1960 at the age of 89. She was just twelve days short of her 90th birthday having survived Edwin by five years. She had a flower named after her and the Emily Grant Hutchings water lily is a beautiful vivid pink hybrid that was produced by George Pring in 1922. Some people claim it to be the brightest coloured water lily under cultivation. A very appropriate tribute to a lady who is, sadly, largely forgotten today.

Emily outlived Lola Hays by more than 40 years. Lola, who was born on August 5th 1866 had her life cut short by heart disease. Her obituary was published in *The Centralia Courier* on January 3rd 1919 stating that she had died on December 31st 1918 aged just 52.

The source of the name Grant is a mystery but was probably a pseudonym Emily used in her writing career. Her death certificate showed that senility and malnutrition contributed to her death. She was cremated but it appears that her remains are unclaimed and lie in storage at Valhalla Cemetery in St Louis, Missouri. In a strange twist of fate, the Find-a-Grave website asks anyone interested in claiming the remains to contact the cemetery.

Mrs Chan-Toon (1873–1940)

Oscar Wilde provided rich pickings for literary forgers, especially in the 1920s, and these clouded the issue over what was genuine and what was skulduggery. A man named Dorian Hope, along with a Mrs Chan-Toon, sought to profit from a pseudo-relationship with Wilde. Although not directly concerned with automatic writing, a brief summary of her life is worth the short diversion.

She was born Mary Mabel Agnes Cosgrove in Cork, Ireland on May 12th 1873 and grew up in London. She was first married to Chan-Toon, the nephew of the King of Burma in 1893 not long after Chan-Toon had been appointed First Judge in the Court of Small Cases at Rangoon. He published a number of textbooks on law from 1894 to 1902. Mabel Cosgrove had already published her first novel under her maiden name in 1892 and went on to produce a collection of short stories entitled *Told on the Pagoda* (1895), and a novel, *Under Eastern Skies* (1901). However, the marriage between them does not appear to have lasted and the couple divorced although shortly after, it was noted that she was a widow. She was served with a bankruptcy notice in London in 1907 although at the time it appears that she was living in Killarney, Ireland. Around that time, she travelled to Mexico City by way of New York to write a romantic novel, ostensibly to be based on the life of the people in the cattle and mining districts. Within two days she had been arrested on a charge of blackmail and put in Belim prison in June 1907. She was accompanied by a young Englishman named Armine Wodehouse Pearse. In 1910, Mrs Chan-Toon was receiving orders from the Reading bankruptcy court although the matter was not resolved until at least November 1927. In 1911, Mabel Chan-Toon married Armine Wodehouse Pearse but the marriage was short-lived. Her husband was killed twelve days before the Armistice on October 31st 1918 and was buried in France. Mrs Pearse scraped a living writing for newspapers and magazines but she had not produced a novel since 1914 when *A Shadow of Burmah* was published.

In 1921, Mrs Chan-Toon passed off a complete play, *For Love of the King*, as being Oscar Wilde's work, even to the point of getting *Hutchinson's Magazine* to initially publish it, later to be followed by Methuen. She even had the temerity to include a letter purported to have come from Wilde many years before regarding the play. In fact, she had taken the plot from one of her own short stories that had been published some twenty years earlier in *The Idler* magazine in April 1900.

In December 1925, she stole £240 from an elderly, illiterate woman called Bridget Wood and absconded to Killarney, Ireland. She was arrested but only £98 remained of the money and she was sent to prison for six months. Shortly after being released, her dark literary past finally caught up with her when a court case between Methuen and the Hampstead bookseller Christopher Millard (1872–1927) revealed *For Love of the King* to be a forgery. Millard, using the name Stuart Mason, was a bibliographer of Oscar Wilde and had been involved in buying and selling doubtful 'Wilde' manuscripts from the bookdealer William Figgis in 1922. Items that Figgis had bought from a conman known as Dorian (or Sebastian) Hope. This was the pseudonym of either Fabien Lloyd (Oscar Wilde's nephew) or was the invention of an American poet named Brett Holland (1898–1934). An article from the Sunday Times dated July 8th 2007 attempted to clarify the matter. What happened to Mrs Chan-Toon (or Pearse) after that is largely unknown. Her mother, Clara, died in Kingston, Surrey in 1910, and her father, Edward, soon after, in 1913. Two family trees on the Ancestry website state that she died in Fulham in 1940. As this was at the time of the London Blitz during World War 2, perhaps this is all we will ever know. Another possibility is that she returned to Killarney in Ireland.

There again, Wilde himself was not above profiteering falsely from his own name. His signed author's editions always fetched a higher price than their standard counterparts and his friend Maurice Gilberts was known to have signed some of the books on Wilde's behalf, especially *The Ballad of Reading Gaol* (1898).

Pearl Curran (1883–1937)

A particularly complex case is the one surrounding Pearl Curran. She was born Pearl Lenore Pollard on February 18th 1883 in Mound City, Illinois. She produced many books of fiction and poetry which she said had been channelled to her by the spirit of a woman named Patience Worth. Pearl and her friend Emily Grant Hutchings occasionally used a Ouija board and the contact began on July 8th 1913 with 'Many moons ago I lived. Again I come. Patience Worth my name. Wait, I would speak with thee. If thou shalt live, then so shall I. I make my bread at thy hearth. Good friends, let us be merrie. The time for work is past. Let the tabby drowse and blink her wisdom to the firelog.' Pearl Curran was given the dates 1649 and 1694 and that Patience came from Portesham in Dorset, England, had emigrated to Nantucket Island, and been killed in a raid by Native Americans. As time passed, the Ouija board became superfluous and Pearl would recite Patience's words freely without going into a trance and unaffected by interruptions. For Pearl, Patience's words were accompanied by the visualisations of people and places and together they wrote *The Sorry Tale*, *Samuel Wheaton*, *Hope Trueblood*, and *Telka*. In fact, the eminent literary critic William Marion Reedy heaped praise on *The Sorry Tale*, describing it as a modern classic. Other novels also appeared, along with some short stories and a large amount of poetry. Remarkably, it was Patience Worth who was named as one of the outstanding authors of 1918, rather than Pearl Curran.

Interest in the writings was fuelled by the revival of Spiritualism that was occurring in the United Kingdom and the United States at the time. In 1848, three sisters, Margaret, Kate, and Leah Fox, had claimed to have contacted a deceased salesman at their home in New York State and this led to the birth of Spiritualism in America, although it went into decline following the Civil War of 1861–1865.

When her husband John Curran died in 1922, she lost her meticulous record keeper and the writing sessions became spasmodic and in the 1920s, her work became unfashionable. She married twice more but neither marriage lasted long. She moved to Los Angeles in 1930. Her last communication from Patience was on November 25th 1937, having received the information from her that her life was nearing its end. In spite of being in good health at the time, by the end of November, Pearl had contracted pneumonia and died on December 3rd 1937 aged just 54.

Many scientists and sceptics have tried to prove that Pearl was a fraud and that Patience was a fictitious creation but nobody has ever achieved this. One of their greatest objections was that one of the novels was set in

Victorian times, two centuries later than Patience's time period but I don't feel that this is any justification for deriding and dismissing the work. The writings contain an in-depth knowledge of the flora and social history of several time periods stretching back many centuries and she was able to draw upon this knowledge without any doubt or hesitation. The case remains one of the most thought provoking mysteries of all time and an explanation has never been forthcoming.

In 2011, the psychologist Richard Wiseman gave the opinion that the messages did not confirm the existence of life after death. Indeed, researchers have failed to uncover any proof that Patience Worth existed in real life although this is hardly a surprise owing to the fact that genealogical records were sketchy in the 17th century. The period does throw up some county Poll Books plus the Censuses of 1801 and 1821 but it was not until the Births and Deaths Registration Act 1836 and the first major census of 1841, that precise records were maintained. Before then, we have little but parish registers to go on unless you were in the higher echelons of society.

Since Pearl Curran's death in 1937, many people have had to concede that her amazing output was likely to have sprung from her subconscious mind rather than any external forces but I do not believe that even if this were true that it would derail or divert interest in the case. Sadly, having amassed nearly four million words between 1913 and 1937, her work is largely unknown today.

There may be a small clue to the whole affair. In 1920, Pearl Curran had begun publishing stories under her own name. *The Saturday Evening Post* paid her $350 for the story *Rosa Alvaro, Entrante* in which a girl named Mayme, who works as a clerk in a Chicago department store (a job that Curran held before marriage) is convinced by a fortune teller that her spirit guide is a beautiful Spanish woman named Rosa Alvaro and the girl begins to live the part of the Spanish noblewoman. The Goldwyn Film Company turned the story into the 54-minute silent film *What Happened to Rosa*, released in December 1920.

Fernando Pessoa (1888–1935)

Fernando Pessoa was a Portuguese writer, poet, philosopher, and commercial translator. He was born Fernando António Nogueira Pessoa on June 13th 1888 at 4 São Carlos Square in Lisbon, Portugal.

His early education was at the Roman Catholic St Joseph Convent School. At the age of five, Fernando's father died and in 1896, his mother took him to South Africa where his stepfather was the Portuguese consul in what was then Natal. He attended the Durban High School in April 1899, where his main influences were the major English classic poets. Apart from a period of nearly fourteen months over 1901–1902, he did not return permanently to Lisbon until August 1905, after which he was influenced by French symbolists and Portuguese poets. Later, he became inspired by other writers, such as TS Eliot, Ezra Pound, James Joyce, and WB Yeats. In 1906, he began studies at the University of Lisbon but dropped out after less than a year when a strike by the students interrupted his classes.

He then worked as a commercial translator and started to publish his own poetry, prose, and literary criticism and contributed material to many newspapers and journals.

From 1912–1914, he lived with his 'Aunt Anica' who held 'semi-spiritualist sessions' at her home but other members of the group described him as a 'delaying element'. However, his interest in Spiritualism was revived in 1915 while translating books on theosophy and by March 1916, he had started to produce automatic writing, considered himself to be a medium, and claimed to have had visions. During the series of automatic writing sessions using a planchette, he communicated with Henry More (1614–1687) the best known of 'The Cambridge Platonists' and other characters such as 'Wardour' and 'The Voodooist'. He described his experiences as 'sometimes suddenly being owned by something else' or having a strange sensation in his right arm, which spontaneously rose into the air. Some of the automatic writings were difficult to understand and often took the form of answers to questions presumably intimated by Pessoa himself. His questions often received anonymous replies and these could be in the form of drawings and numbers related to the Kabbalah and to Freemasonry. He became a competent astrologer and studied many aspects of the occult including alchemy, numerology, and hermeticism. His writing was also influenced by Rosicrucianism and theosophy.

Pessoa was a prolific writer and wrote under many pseudonyms although he preferred to call them heteronyms because each of them possessed their own independent existence, intellect, and opinions. He created at least 75 heteronyms but his main literary alter egos were Alberto Caeiro (an uneducated poet), Álvaro de Campos (a well-travelled naval engineer) and Ricardo Reis (an unhappy doctor devoted to classic themes). These three, in particular, were fully formed individuals who possessed their own literary styles which allowed them to criticise and comment on each other's work. The heteronyms, with their complex biographies, contribute in no small way to the fascination surrounding Pessoa's work, which has only received due recognition in recent years. Pessoa stated that he saw the heteronyms several times when looking in a mirror and that his face faded and was replaced by theirs. Conventional religion did not interest him and though he opposed the idea of 'spirit writing' there is little doubt that the methods by which he received his heteronymic outpourings bore every resemblance to the automatic writings received by other mediums. Pessoa was beset by doubts about his sanity for much of his life but there is no evidence that he suffered from schizophrenia or multiple personality disorder.

After his death, a large wooden trunk was discovered containing more than 25,000 items that represented his lifetime's work. The writings included typed manuscripts, backs of envelopes, scraps of paper, and innumerable fragments of material. They covered the subjects of history, philosophy, sociology, fiction, plays, as well as works related to astrology and literary criticism. Scattered among the wealth of manuscripts were the hundreds of items that form *Livro do Desassossego* (Book of Disquiet), which Pessoa claimed was the work of Bernardo Soares, one of his semi-heteronyms. Possibly his greatest work, it was not published until 1982, since when many translations and versions have become available. A guidebook to Lisbon that he wrote in 1925 also had a long wait and it was eventually published in 1992. He published three volumes of poetry in English, *Antinous* (1918), *Sonnets* (1918), and *English Poems* (1921). The only book in Portuguese that he published during his lifetime was *Mensagem* (Message) (1934), a collection of poetry that created a mythology based on Portugal's heroic past.

On November 29th 1935, Pessoa was admitted to hospital with a fever and abdominal pain. That day, he wrote in English 'I know not what tomorrow will bring'. He died at 8pm the following evening, November 30th 1935, aged 47. The cause of death was not conclusive but is usually given as cirrhosis of the liver, pancreatitis, or hepatitis, any of which would have been exacerbated by his alcoholism. He was buried at the Cemitério dos Prazeres but in 1985, his remains were moved to the Hieronymites Monastery, where Luís de Camões and Vasco da Gama are also buried. Pessoa's home for the last fifteen years of his life is now the Fernando Pessoa Museum at 16 Rua Coelho da Rocha, Campo de Ourique, Lisbon.

Mina Crandon (1889–1941)

During the 1920s, Arthur Conan Doyle lectured across America on his advocacy of Spiritualism and one of the mediums he endorsed was Mina 'Margery' Crandon. She produced automatic writing in foreign languages such as Japanese and Chinese and though this was a lesser part of her mediumship, she is worthy of mention. Born Mina Margeurite Stinson on August 28th 1889 in North Marysburgh, Prince Edward Island, Ontario, she was still a teenager when she moved to Boston, Massachusetts to pursue her love of music. She played several instruments in various orchestras and dance bands before working as a secretary, actress, and as an ambulance driver. Her first marriage to Earl Rand having failed she became the third wife of Dr Le Roi Goddard Crandon (1873–1939). He was a wealthy Boston surgeon and they lived at 10 Lime Street in the Beacon Hill district in Boston. Within a few years of her marriage to Crandon, he introduced her to the paranormal practice of 'table tipping'. In May 1923, they invited four friends to their elegant four-storey house and held a séance in a small room on the top floor. Mina continued to experiment with séances in the company of impressionable family and friends, partly owing to her husband's morbid fear of death.

During her sittings in the pitch blackness of the narrow room, the sitters would experience flashes of light, bumps, bangs, and disembodied voices. Sometimes, a Victrola (wind-up phonograph) would spontaneously start and stop. Mina claimed that she could channel messages from her brother who had died twelve years earlier and Walter Stinson became a regular 'visitor' to the séances.

She had no apparent paranormal ability and did not look for fame and fortune. However, she was thrust into the limelight when her mediumship fell under the gaze of the magazine *Scientific American*. They had put up a $5,000 prize for any medium who could demonstrate telekinesis in controlled conditions but had not made any positive progress after more than a year. Mina's name was put forward on June 23rd 1924 and Conan Doyle's backing and her own absence of concern for personal gain made her a credible candidate. The couple had no need for the prize money and merely saw the competition as an opportunity to gain approval of Mina's mediumship. She became known as 'Margery' after asking J Malcolm Bird, an associate editor of the *Scientific American*, to protect her name prior to their investigations. The prize committee included Harry Houdini and they observed sessions at the Crandons' home at 10 Lime Street, Boston in July 1924 followed by more attendances a month later. Using a variety of constraints, they subjected Margery to all manner of tests using galvanometers etc but the committee could not agree on the validity of her work, even after nearly 100 séances. Houdini, who had devised a cabinet that restricted her movements, was angry at their failure to unanimously condemn Margery as a fraud and explained in detail how she had created the 'paranormal' events. Houdini even re-created the events as a part of his stage act and produced a booklet explaining her trickery. In 1925, the *Scientific American* committee finally stated that their investigation was over and Margery was denied the prize but that was not quite the end of their involvement with the paranormal. As late as 1941, the prize was still on offer and had risen to $15,000.

In June 1925, a committee composed of Harvard University scholars also declared Margery to be a fraud after observing her draw objects from her lap, one of which purported to be a hand which was later revealed by biologists to be shaped from a piece of animal liver. This 'hand' only appeared and disappeared when her husband was sat next to her.

She was also investigated by the American Society for Psychical Research in 1926. Three professors deduced that the 'ectoplasm' exuding from Margery's mouth was nothing more than a thin rod covered in soft leather.

She would often host her séances scantily clad, wearing just a thin gown, silk stockings and slippers. Many of Margery's séances were performed in the nude. She would occasionally sprinkle luminous powder on her breasts and was said to have sat on the laps of her male sitters. Dr Sandon was clearly complicit in these arrangements because he would sometimes display nude photographs of her mediumship sessions. Dr Crandon is reputed to have persuaded Mina to sometimes conduct séances against her wishes and she became resentful towards the end of her life.

After her husband's death in 1939 and fuelled by depression, a suicide attempt failed when she tried to leap from the roof of the house during a séance but her alcohol addiction did prove fatal and she died in Boston on November 1st 1941, aged just 51.

In a 2013 interview, Mina's great granddaughter, Anna Thurlow, said 'I certainly do not see her as a victim, however. I think one thing that has gotten lost in the written history is that what she produced in the séances was often quite beautiful, and fun. She took on an intellectual challenge and certainly gave the investigators a great show. I would like to think that she derived some sense of satisfaction from that.'

Geraldine Cummins (1890–1969)

The wives of Conan Doyle and Yeats were not alone in having their authorship ignored. It was common practice not to credit the mediums, most of whom were women, and usually the clients' or male family member's names appeared on title pages. In the Victorian era, women were viewed as being blank slates upon which the spirits could write their message and that men were considered to be 'in charge' and better suited to the business side of things. As Spiritualism became more socially acceptable, educated and intelligent women who were traditionally short of opportunity saw it as a means of entering the world of publishing in their own right.

One automatic writer, Geraldine Dorothy Cummins, was prominent in taking a stand against being sidelined by men and her actions resulted in the law of copyright being changed. She was born in Cork, Ireland on January 24th 1890, played hockey for Ireland, and joined the suffragette movement, making a number of speeches in support of the cause. Her early career included co-writing three plays for the Abbey Theatre in Dublin in the years leading up to World War One. She wrote several novels including a study of working class life in Ireland titled *The Land They Loved* (1919) and *The Fires of Beltane* (1936), both of which demonstrated her involvement with feminist issues. Geraldine's interest was drawn to psychic phenomena and she met the Irish spiritualist medium Hester Dowden (1868–1949) during a visit to Paris in June 1914. An intriguing Ouija board session with Hester encouraged Geraldine to leave Cork and take up a job at the National Library of Ireland in Dublin. She rented a room in Hester Dowden's house and it was there that her mediumship began. Not long afterwards, one of her first sitters was WB Yeats who, along with Bram Stoker, was one of Hester's social circle of friends. In October 1924, she received quite detailed messages from George Mallory who disappeared on the June 1924 Everest expedition when he and Sandy Irvine were making an attempt to reach the summit. If the account is to be believed, the pair never actually made it to the top.

In 1923, she met a wealthy psychic investigator, Miss Edith Beatrice Gibbes, who would become a regular companion and compiler of her automatic writings. Geraldine went to London and lived with Gibbes at 25 Jubilee Place, Chelsea where she was given a life interest in the property. It was there that she started to produce her biblical automatic writing scripts. Her first psychic book was *The Spirits of Cleophas* (1928), followed by *Paul in Athens* (1930) and *The Great Days of Ephesus* (1933). They formed *The Chronicles of Cleophas* and were said to supplement the *Acts of the Apostles* and the *Epistles of St Paul*, following the crucifixion of Jesus. Cleophas was said to have used at least seven 'messengers' to pass on the information to Geraldine. During the production of the first book, she was accompanied by the architect Frederick Bligh Bond but after that she received the text independently. Although her normal writing speed was quite measured, her spirit writing created words at the rate of nearly 2,000 words per hour. Bond tried to publish the book himself but in July 1926, Geraldine took Bond to court over the matter and he had to attend the High Court of Justice. Bond stated that being the sitter, he owned the messages because they were given to him and that he had typed them up. He added that Geraldine 'could not have produced the work if he had not cooperated by placing his hand on the back of hers during the writing', notwithstanding the fact that she persistently tried to remove it. This led to a landmark ruling over who owned the copyright to automatic or spirit writing. The judge, Justice Eve, was not without a sense of humour and stated that he had no jurisdiction on the spiritual plane and that his judgement was limited to England. Geraldine won the case when Cummins v. Bond set a precedent by ruling that the author must be human because without their transcription, the work would not exist.

Several theologians attended her sessions and her editors recognised the literary value of the biblical content of the books saying that it threw new light on the *Acts of the Apostles*. They considered that the books contained information more in keeping with a student of the early church yet Geraldine neither studied religious belief nor visited the Holy Land.

In 1931, she became very ill with cancer yet managed to work on her fourth book *The Road to Immortality* (1932). This is probably the most famous 'other world' communication ever produced, supposedly received from the long deceased Frederic William Henry Myers (1843–1901). Myers, who was a founder of the Society for Psychical Research in 1883, gave an astounding view of the afterlife and described humanity's spiritual enlightenment and evolution on its journey through eternity.

T E Lawrence (Lawrence of Arabia) died in a motorcycle accident in 1935 and he contacted Geraldine six months after the event on two occasions. He spoke of his discomfort in the company of women and explained why he had changed his name to Shaw and why he sought anonymity in his later years.

In the 1940s and 1950s, she worked with doctors on a project that employed Spiritualism to treat mental illness through the exploration of the subconscious mind. In collaboration with a psychiatrist who called himself 'R Connell', she explored these theories in *Perceptive Healing* (1945) and *Healing the Mind* (1957).

There is a fascinating period in her life that has never been explained. In Charles Fryer's biography *Geraldine Cummins: An Appreciation* (1990), he writes that from 1940 to 1944, she was 'doing some work of an investigative nature which involved her in a certain amount of danger and was undertaken from patriotic motives'. Eric Robertson Dodds, who had spoken to Geraldine shortly before she died, stated that she had told him that she had been working as a British agent in Ireland. Apparently, this undercover work involved the investigation of German sympathisers in the IRA. Her cover, as an innocent medium, was perfect from a non-political standpoint and many of the papers she left when she died have never been released by the government. Fryer himself also experienced automatic writing from 1971 and it encouraged him to research Geraldine's life.

She did publish her own literature in later years including the play *Till Yesterday Comes Again* (1938) which was produced by the Chanticleer Theatre, London and *Variety Show* (1959), a collection of short stories. She published her autobiography *Unseen Adventures* (1951) in which she explained how she placed more value on being a medium than in pursuit of politics and women's suffrage. Amusingly, she recalled the occasion when she gave a talk to an unusually full audience in Brighton owing to a misprint in the publicity material. Advertised as *The Road to Immorality*, it gave the impression of a rather more adventurous talk than Geraldine had in mind.

She published a biography of writer and spiritualist Edith Somerville *Dr E AE Somerville, A Biography* (1952). She also wrote *The Fate of Colonel Fawcett* (1955) based on messages that she said had come from the missing explorer Percy H Fawcett (1867–1925) who disappeared in the Brazilian jungle. She received messages from Fawcett in 1925 and 1936 when he reported that he was still alive, and in 1948 from his spirit reporting his death. Automatic writers naturally attract accusations of fraud and Geraldine was no exception. Doubters will point out that both Cummins and Fawcett contributed articles to *The Occult Review* and suggest that her writings were drawn from her own subliminal memory and subconscious. Regardless of the origins of her automatic writing, Geraldine's sincerity was never in question even though she herself never accepted the writing at face value.

Her last book, *Swan on a Black Sea: A Study in Automatic Writing: The Cummins-Willett Scripts* (1965) was a detailed account of the scripts she received from the spirit of 'Mrs Willett' which was the spiritualist name of Winifred Coombe Tennant (1874–1956). Geraldine's health deteriorated in the mid-1960s and she returned to her home town of Cork where she was advised to set aside the world of the psychic for the good of her health. Geraldine never married and was Ireland's most celebrated psychic. In spite of the scepticism with which she viewed the communications that she received, she was never considered to be less than genuine. She died on August 25th 1969 and is buried in St Lappans in Cork. Her gravestone is quite obscure and gives no indication of her incredible life.

André Breton (1896–1966)

André Breton was born on February 19th 1896 in Tinchebray, France. He studied psychiatry at medical school and in World War 1 worked in neurological wards in Nantes. A later meeting with Sigmund Freud in 1921 sparked his interest in psychoanalysis and the concept of the unconscious.

Automatic writing was a significant element of the Surrealist movement. The term 'surrealism' is said to have been first used by Guillaume Apollinaire in 1917 although the Surrealist movement was officially established on October 15th 1924 when its founder, André Breton, published the Surrealist Manifesto in Paris. According to the Manifesto, 'Surrealism is the dictation of thought in the absence of all control exercised by reason, outside of all aesthetic and moral preoccupation.' A natural successor to Dadaism, wherein its roots may be found, Surrealism became known as both a cultural and revolutionary movement with links to anarchism and communism. It spread quickly around the world from its roots in Paris, making a huge impact on the arts, politics, and philosophy of many countries.

In the early days, Breton concentrated on automatic writing in his attempts to access a higher plane of existence but much of the writing that he produced by what he termed 'pure psychic automatism' was heavily edited and he began to place more emphasis on the visual arts. Artists and writers developed techniques whereby they could allow the unconscious to express itself through their artwork and literature.

The Surrealists typically held their meetings in cafés, where they played drawing games to stimulate creativity and began to experiment with both automatic drawing and writing as a means of expressing the subconscious. Writing as quickly as possible, the absence of conscious thought was often central to the material that its members produced. Unfortunately, very few of these writing experiments survive today. In 1925, they created 'The Exquisite Corpse', a game in which three artists each created one third of a drawing without knowing what the others had drawn. The game was so called because the final result was meant to resemble an image of the human body. The contributors only knew which part of the body was their responsibility and last two artists were able to view a small part of where the first artist had finished. The Surrealists believed that chance and the collective unconscious could coincide and enable them to create mysterious and surprising works of art. One of the most famous surrealist works is Breton's refined poetic novel *Soluble Fish* (1924). Another of his important theoretical works is *The Automatic Message* (1933) which dealt with automatism. Breton died in Paris on September 28th 1966.

Phillippe Soupault (1897–1990)

Philippe Soupault was a French poet and novelist and was born on August 2nd 1897 in Chaville, France. He supported Dadaism and was instrumental in the creation of the Surrealist movement.

Soupault's earliest collection of poetry *Aquarium* (1917) was published with the help of Guillaume Apollinaire who introduced Soupault to André Breton. In 1919, Soupault, Breton, and Louis Aragon co-founded the Dadaist review *Littérature*. In 1920, Breton and Soupault published *Les Champs magnétiques* (The Magnetic Fields). It was the first example of literary surrealism and was created by means of automatic writing. The text was often nonsensical but was considered superior to other surrealist techniques such as 'The Exquisite Corpse' where each member of a group would add images or words to a composition in turn and each new day would be the start of a new chapter.

In 1922, Soupault was invited to redesign the literary magazine *Les Écrits nouveaux* and in 1927 his wife Marie-Louise helped him to translate William Blake's *Songs of Innocence and Experience* into French. Soupault soon gave up automatic writing and concentrated on his poetry. He became unhappy with the Surrealist movement and left, breaking his links with Breton.

From the mid-1920s, Soupault concentrated on writing novels and essays, and journalism. His novels, which took revolution and freedom as their themes, included *Les Frères Durandeau* (The Durandeau Brothers) (1924), *Le Nègre* (The Negro) (1927), and *Les Moribonds* (The Dying) (1934).

In 1933, he met the photographer Ré Richter at the Soviet embassy in Paris. They travelled across Europe as photo-journalists and married in 1937. His involvement with Radio Tunis from 1937 to 1940 led to six months imprisonment by the Nazis but he and Ré then travelled to the United States via Algiers. Philippe returned to France in October 1945 although Ré remained in New York. He wrote about his prison experiences in *Le Temps des assassins* (Age of Assassins) (1945). After World War 2, Soupault directed the overseas broadcasts of Radio Television Francaise (RTF) and worked in broadcasting until the 1970s. *Mémoires de l'oubli* (Memoirs of Oblivion) (1981) was his last published work.

In later years, Philippe and Ré were reunited and collaborated on various projects including *Märchen aus fünf Kontinenten* (Fairy Tales from Five Continents) (1968) and a television film about Wassily Kandinsky in 1967. From the early 1970s, they shared a house together. Phillippe Soupault died at his home in Paris on March 12th 1990 aged 92. Ré outlived him by five years, dying on March 12th 1996 in Versailles aged 94.

Les Automatistes

In the early 1940s, the French-Canadian painter Paul-Émile Borduas founded the dissident movement Les Automatistes. Inspired by the writings of André Breton, Borduas created unplanned, spontaneous gouache paintings based on automatic drawing and exhibited 45 of them at the Ermitage Théâtre in Montréal in April 1942. This attracted a following from students at the École des beaux-arts, the École du Meuble. and the Collège Notre-Dame and they met in Borduas's studio to consider Surrealism and Marxism. Members of the group included Marcel Barbeau, Claude and Pierre Gauvreau, Jean-Paul Riopelle, Roger Fauteux, Fernand Leduc, Jean-Paul Mousseau, Marcelle Ferron, and Françoise Sullivan. Based on Surrealist principles and their stream of consciousness approach, they held their first Montreal exhibition in April 1946. At their second in February 1947, they received a review by the journalist Tancrède Marcil Jr in which he designated them as 'Automatistes', taking the name from the Surrealists' concept of automatism. The group held significant exhibitions in New York (1946) and Paris (1947) and they began to extend their interest to poetry, drama, and dance. In August 1948, Borduas published the group manifesto *Refus Global* (Total Refusal), expressing the Automatistes' political and religious views. The sixteen signatories put their names to an anti-establishment and anti-religious document that totally rejected the social and artistic values of Québéc society. In their declaration of artistic and expressive freedoms, their denunciation of the authority of the Catholic Church was particularly withering. It criticized the 'cassocks that have remained the sole repositories of faith, knowledge, truth, and national wealth' and argued against the existence of God.

The group dispersed soon after the manifesto was published. Borduas lost his job at the École du meuble de Montréal where he had been teaching since 1937 and had to move to New York. Their last exhibition, 'La Matière Chante' took place in 1954.

Although only half of the 400 printed copies of *Refus Global* were sold, the manifesto caused uproar, remains an important work in Quebec's cultural history, and is widely seen to have been one of the precursors to its 'Quiet Revolution'.

Francisco 'Chico' Xavier (1910–2002)

Francisco 'Chico' Xavier was born on April 2nd 1910 in Pedro Leopoldo, Minas Gerais, Brazil. He was arguably the most prolific automatic writer in history, producing more than 490 books and several thousand letters over a period of more than 60 years. His psychic abilities became apparent at the age of four. When he was five, his mother died and he claimed to be able to talk with her spirit for several years afterwards. At school he won an essay competition, stating that he received the text of all his essays from a spirit but nobody paid much attention to him. At the age of twelve he was accused of plagiarism and it was a problem that haunted him throughout his life. He had to finish education early in order to help support his family yet was able to produce books that appeared to far surpass his academic abilities.

In 1928, he published his first automatic messages in the newspapers *O Jornal* (Rio de Janeiro) and *Almanaque de Notícias* (Portugal).

His book *Parnaso de Além-Túmulo* (Parnassus Beyond the Tomb) (1931) made him famous in Brazil. It contained 259 poems that he said had been received from 56 dead Brazilian and Portuguese poets. In the same year, he had his first communication from his spirit guide Emmanuel. Xavier later discovered that Emmanuel had also lived as Publius Lentulus (a Roman Senator), Manuel da Nóbrega (an 18th century Jesuit priest), Father Damien (from Spain), and as a professor at the Sorbonne.

In 1959, he moved to Uberaba which led to the town becoming a place of pilgrimage. He was already known for the vast number of spirit messages that he had received that had given comfort to the families of deceased family members and thousands of people arrived every day in the hope that Xavier would give them spirit messages from their own dead relatives. In 1975, he founded the spiritist centre 'Casa da Prece' in Uberaba.

His published works covered a huge variety of subjects, including science, philosophy, poetry, religion, literature, and fiction. He never benefited personally from his writings, donating the proceeds from 50 million books to charity. His appearances on television chat shows in the 1960s and 1970s initiated renewed interest in the Brazilian philosophy 'Spiritism Doctrine', attracting in excess of five million devotees. Like most spiritists, he never felt the need to provide any proof of his abilities and his supporters point to the sheer volume and literary quality of his writings as being testimony enough. In spite of being troubled by poor health for the last 30 years of his life, Xavier was still working up to his death aged 92 on June 30th 2002 in Uberaba, Minas Gerais. The film *Chico Xavier* (2010) was based on the biography *As Vidas de Chico Xavier* (1994) by Marcel Souto Maior.

Ruth Montgomery (1912–2001)

Nothing in her early life or career in journalism gave any indication that she would eventually develop psychic abilities, especially as her first literary encounter with psychic phenomena happened in the mid-1950s when she investigated the world of fraudulent mediums. She exposed them in a series of newspaper articles but by 1965, she herself was a strong believer in the afterlife and the world of spirit. During the 1960s and 1970s, Ruth Montgomery became a household name when her automatic writing became the foundation for a series of books on life after death and reincarnation.

Ruth Shick Montgomery was born Ruth Whitmer Schick in Sumner, Illinois on June 11th 1912. She was educated at Baylor and Purdue Universities before embarking on a long and distinguished career in journalism. Whilst still at university, she started working as a cub reporter for the *Waco News Tribune* before working full time for the *Louisville Herald-Post*. In 1935, she married Robert Hiram Montgomery, a businessman from Detroit and worked for the *Detroit News* and the *Chicago Tribune* before joining the *New York Daily News* in 1943 as their first female Washington DC correspondent. At Franklin D Roosevelt's funeral on April 14th 1945, she was the only female reporter of the twelve invited to be present. Ruth's political reporting took her around the world and her coverage of foreign affairs included the Berlin Airlift of 1948–1949, an interview with Juan Peron shortly after he came to power, and she was on the ground in Cuba and Egypt when their leaders were toppled by massive political upheavals.

Beginning in 1952, Ruth wrote an annual newspaper column which listed predictions of world events that the psychic Jeane Dixon had seen in her crystal ball.

In 1956, Ruth became a Washington D.C. correspondent for the International News Service and her newspaper columns were syndicated to 200 newspapers across the country.

Around 1958, she met up with the renowned psychic medium Arthur Augustus Ford (1896–1971) when he visited Washington to give a speech about his plans for a new organization called the Spiritual Frontiers Fellowship. After his talk, she succeeded in getting an interview with him for her column which went out in the Sunday editions. Later on, Ford, who was to become her mentor, told her that she had the ability to receive automatic writing and it was not long before it arrived, enabling her to communicate with various deceased people. She was soon able to receive the communications via a typewriter instead of pencil and paper and most of her psychic experiences relied upon automatic writing received from her spiritual guides from other worlds.

She was a regular at White House press conferences and was a member of Vice President Richard Nixon's press corps on his trip to the U.S.S.R. and Poland in August 1959. Shortly after Nixon became the U.S. President in 1969, Ruth retired from her journalism career and lived in Mexico with her husband for a time where she became a believer in the existence of extra-terrestrial contact and wrote about her encounters with non-human aliens. After Mexico they retired, first to Virginia Beach and then later to Florida.

In 1962, Ruth began to focus on writing books. She published three books about her experiences of working with various presidents in Washington DC, *Mrs. L.B.J.* (1964), *Flowers at the White House* (1967), and *Hail to the Chiefs; My Life and Times with Six Presidents* (1970). Ruth also wrote eleven books on the supernatural and her book *Once There was a Nun: Mary McCarran's Years as Sister Mary Mercy* (1962) began her long career as a non-fiction author. Her biography of the spirit medium Jeane Dixon, *A Gift of Prophecy* (1965), sold more than three million copies and she started to look more closely at paranormal phenomena. The book described Dixon's prediction in 1956 of the assassination of President John F Kennedy. Jeane had warned Kennedy not to visit Dallas and told her friends on the morning of November 22nd 1963 'this is the day it will happen.' The book also mentioned Jeane's prediction a week before the actual event that Robert F Kennedy would be assassinated in 1968. Ruth Montgomery did have doubts about Jeane Dixon's clairvoyance. She complained that the editors of the book 'insisted on deleting most of my references to Jeane Dixon's many wrong predictions, leaving in mainly those on which she had hit correctly'. As a result of this, John Allen Paulos coined the term 'the Jeane Dixon effect'. Paulos, a mathematics professor at Temple University in Philadelphia who specialised in logic and probability theory, was referring to the endorsement of a few correct predictions whilst disregarding a large number of incorrect ones.

After *The Gift of Prophecy* she wrote ten books on psychic phenomena. From 1960–1969, she was communicating with spirit guides and she worked with 'Lily and the group' to produce *A Search for the Truth* (1967) and *Here and Hereafter* (1968). The books dealt with her own spiritual progress, and karma and reincarnation.

Ruth gave up automatic typewriting in 1969 because she no longer needed it to bolster her beliefs but in 1971, she discovered that the recently deceased Arthur Ford had become one of her guides and she restarted the taking of spirit dictation. The guides, now known as 'Lily, Art and the group' provided the foundation for *A World Beyond* (1971), *Companions Along the Way* (1974), *A World Before / The World Before Us* (1976), and

178

Threshold to Tomorrow (1983). These books discussed life after death, Ruth's previous incarnations, the history of the world, and the near future prospects of humanity.

Also in the late 1970s, Ruth was writing about aliens and UFOs in *Strangers Among Us* (1979) and *Aliens Among Us* (1985).

One of the last books Montgomery wrote was her autobiography *Ruth Montgomery: Herald of a New Age* (1986). Written in collaboration with Joanne Garland, the book covered her journalism career as well as her rise and popularity as a psychic. Her final book was *The Worlds to Come: The Guide's Long-Awaited Predictions for a Dawning Age* (1999) in which she announced her predictions for the future of the planet. They said that Earth would shift on its axis and that its surface would suffer significant change in terms of the sea and the land.

The theory of 'walk-ins' was also popularised by Montgomery. This is the concept that a soul can leave a human body, either temporarily or permanently, because it has finished its mission on earth and another soul might take its place. She also took the view that many prominent people were 'walk-ins'. Her book *Strangers Among Us* dealt extensively with this and saw them as advanced spirit guides who were expected to lead humanity in to a more enlightened age. *Threshold to Tomorrow* expanded on Ruth's ideas about the subject and stated that a person could be a 'walk-in' without knowing it.

She claimed to enjoy psychic conversations with her husband Robert after he died of heart disease in 1993 and following her own death in Naples, Florida from emphysema on June 10th 2001, several psychics have professed to have had spirit contact with her.

Her work paved the way for what is now known as the New Age movement. Montgomery believed that she had a purpose in life, and it was to educate people about the psychic world, the paranormal, reincarnation and other concepts.

In 2007, six years after Ruth's death, the Macomber family from New England published *Ruth Montgomery Writes Again!* based upon automatic writing they claimed to have received from her. The Macombers were alleged to have been told that the book was the first of a series that would instruct humanity in how it can save itself from self-destruction. The book was so badly written and of such doubtful provenance that no further volumes were forthcoming.

Rosemary Brown (1916–2001)

Rosemary Brown was a remarkable composer, pianist, and spirit medium who claimed to have received hundreds of new musical works from deceased composers, much of which remains unpublished. Her remarkable claims have inspired controversy ever since although the compositions were acknowledged by many experts to have shown considerable musical accomplishment.

She was born Rosemary Isabel Dickeson in Stockwell, London on July 27th 1916 and many members of her family were said to be psychic including her parents and grandparents. She grew up in a flat above an assembly or dance hall in Balham and her mother Beatrice was a catering manager who also played the piano occasionally in her spare time. Her father, Frank Dickeson, was variously a plumber and an electrician but his bad temper blighted her childhood. Rosemary was an aspiring ballet dancer but when she left the Rosa Bassett School (a grammar school for girls) her father saw to it that she went to work for the Post Office. In May 1940, during a World War 2 blackout, she was walking home from work when she heard a voice telling her to avoid Balham High Road, her usual route. She duly heeded the advice and escaped a German bombing raid that killed hundreds of people.

When she was seven years old, she had a vision in her home of an old man in a black gown. He had long white hair and told Rosemary that he was a composer and that when she was grown up, he would return and make her famous by giving her some music. At the time, she had no idea who he was but about ten years later she saw a photograph and realised that her visitor had been the Hungarian composer Franz Liszt. Rosemary continued to see the spirits of dead people during her school years but realising she was different to the other children, kept the experiences to herself to avoid attracting attention.

In 1943, she contracted polio but she overcame it although it caused her to have a weakness in her left side. Her father passed away the following year. In 1948, when she was 32, she got a second-hand upright piano and took lessons on and off until 1951.

In 1952, she married a government scientist, Charles Brown, who had once worked as a gardener for King Farouk of Egypt. They had a son and a daughter before Charles died in 1961 after an illness that clouded their lives with poverty. That same year, her mother also died and she began visiting spiritualists and attending New Age circles.

She suffered broken ribs in an accident in 1964 at the school kitchen where she worked and, in March, returned to the piano whilst she was recovering. As he had 'promised' forty years earlier, Franz Liszt renewed his contact with Rosemary and she recognised him immediately. Liszt arranged for other dead composers who wanted to dictate new music through her to come forward. She claimed that his spirit introduced her to many other composers including Bach, Beethoven, Brahms, Chopin, Debussy, Grieg, Mozart, Rachmaninov, Schubert, Schumann, and Stravinsky. They dictated new compositions to her and she transcribed the notes. These works included a 40 page Schubert sonata, a Fantaisie-Impromptu in three movements from Chopin, twelve further songs she attributed to Schubert, and two sonatas and two symphonies she claimed were given to her by Beethoven, including his 10th and 11th symphonies.

She claimed that each composer had his own method of transmission whilst she sat at the piano. Liszt took control of her hands for several bars after which she wrote down the notes. Schubert tried to sing his compositions but 'He hasn't a very good voice' said Rosemary. Chopin told her the notes and pushed her fingers down upon the correct keys. Bach and Beethoven preferred her to take dictation whilst sat at a table. Others simply dictated their new music to Rosemary directly. Rosemary stated that she usually heard the instructions in English but on occasions other languages would be given as notes to the music. Other compositions that arrived on the ether were *Henrietta* by Fats Waller, a piece from Gershwin, and a song by Gracie Fields.

Rosemary claimed that her own musical training had been fairly basic over a period of just a few years. Her own piano skills were competent but modest and she could not play by ear. When she received pieces from the deceased composers, she struggled to keep up as they dictated at considerable speed. The process was laborious and the scribbled early versions of compositions in the archive contain many notes regarding the rules of musical notation and extensive revisions and amendments.

She also described some strange experiences arising from her visitations. When watching television, Chopin was appalled by the technology and when out shopping, Liszt showed an interest in the price of bananas. She said that Debussy wore 'very bizarre clothes' and that Chopin shouted some words in French which she later translated to be a warning that 'her bath was overflowing'.

In 1968, Sir George Trevelyan showed some of Rosemary's work to Mary Firth (1920–2013), a musical director at a college for further education. Mary, along with her husband George Firth and Trevelyan, helped to set up a fund for Rosemary in order that she could give up her usual employment as a school dinner lady and devote all of her time to her music. She accepted the offer but terminated the arrangement after two years because she disliked being under any type of obligation.

In addition to long spiritual sessions which could last for many hours at a time, she had to endure relentless questioning and criticism. Then on May 29th 1969, following an invitation from the BBC, Rosemary was asked to try and receive a spirit composition whilst being interviewed by Peter Dorling in a live television studio for the programme *Mrs Brown and the Great Composers.* She was apprehensive about the chances of success in such circumstances but Liszt stepped forward and gave her a rather lovely piece called *Grübelei* (meditation). Unlike some of her other work which was occasionally described as 'lightweight', *Grübelei* is a spectacular and unusual piece of music. During the programme, Hephzibah Menuhin said about *Grübelei,* 'It is the sort of piece Liszt could well have written, particularly during the last fifteen years of his life'. More generally, a member of the Liszt Society, Vernon Harrison, said that her pieces by Liszt were 'not good enough to carry conviction that they emanate from the sources to which she attributes them but they are too good to dismiss lightly' and he was especially impressed with *Grübelei.*

Her work received incredibly detailed scrutiny and though it was not taken seriously by a sizeable proportion of the music establishment owing to their concerns regarding authenticity, many well-known people supported her. After studying her compositions, some experts concluded, not unreasonably, that her compositions were purely the work of her own subconscious and that the composers were secondary personalities of Rosemary Brown herself.

The British composer Richard Rodney Bennett argued that it would have been impossible for a person of Rosemary's limited talent to produce such music on her own. He said in an interview in *Time* magazine that 'If she is a fake, she is a brilliant one and must have had years of training. Some of the music is awful, but some is marvellous. I couldn't have faked the Beethoven.' Like Bennett, Leonard Bernstein was also impressed, especially by her Rachmaninov and Chopin pieces, but doubtful about her claims. Critics pointed out the similarity of some of the musical forms, the repetition of melodic sequences, and that parts of the notation lacked the characteristics of their supposed composers. Andre Previn was also less than complimentary when he said that 'If the newly found compositions were genuine, they would best have been left on the shelf.'

Rosemary countered objections by explaining that her visitors often laid out only the main themes in the works and that she, with her considerably lesser skills, had to fill in the missing parts of them. She was often asked about some of the famous cases of unfinished works such as Schubert's *Symphony in B Minor* (D. 759). She recalled that she had 'actually heard the end of the Unfinished Symphony and it is very, very beautiful' but unfortunately the composer never dictated the music to her.

Rosemary was regarded by some as being a fraud or self-deluded but the composer and musicologist Ian Parrott argued in her favour and wrote in her 2001 Guardian obituary that she was 'a modest, sincere and utterly genuine musical medium'.

Her spiritual connections were not confined to music. She claimed to have been in contact with the spirits of Shakespeare, Einstein, GB Shaw, Jung and Bertrand Russell. This would have come as a surprise to Russell for in his essay *Do We Survive Death?,* he had come down in favour of the negative. George Bernard Shaw went so far as to present her with two plays, *The Heavenly Maze* and *Caesar's Revenge*, which was performed at the Edinburgh Fringe Festival in 1978. Her literary landscape was littered with poetry dictated by John Betjeman, William Blake, Rupert Brooke, Edward Lear, Elizabeth Barrett Browning, Emily Bronte, Keats, Shelley, Coleridge, and Wordsworth. In her later years, other non-musicians made an appearance, including Diana Dors and Douglas Bader.

She toured Europe and made several appearances on BBC Radio and BBC TV from 1969 onwards. In the United States, she played at New York Town Hall and appeared on *The Tonight Show* with Johnny Carson and on *The Oscar Petersen Show*. She performed in London at venues such as the Wigmore Hall, the Purcell Room, and the Queen Elizabeth Hall.

She made a number of recordings until 1988 although by the mid-1980s, her visits by deceased composers had already ceased owing to her declining health.

The distinguished concert pianists Robin Stone, Peter Katin, Philip Gammon, Howard Shelley, Cristina Ortiz, and John Lill have all performed her music.

Brown was the subject of a BBC Radio 4 drama, *The Lambeth Waltz* by Daniel Thurman, first broadcast in 2017.

It is not widely known that Rosemary also attended art classes and later revealed that she had received guidance from artists such as William Blake, JMW Turner, and Vincent van Gogh. In a BBC documentary, she showed some psychic paintings she claimed to have created when these past masters guided her hands. Although mere pastiches of the deceased artists' styles, they are yet another example of the extraordinary output of this amazing woman.

In the semi-fictional novel *Ghost Variations* (1916) by Jessica Duchen, Schumann, by way of a Ouija board, reveals information to the Hungarian violinist Jelly d'Aranyi about his missing violin concerto. With interest in the fictional accounts of composers' afterlives gaining ground, perhaps it is time to revive national interest in Rosemary Brown's amazing life. Whatever stance one takes regarding the validity of the work, including the fact that she only channelled white male composers, it surely raises fascinating although naturally unanswerable questions regarding the whole subject of divine musical transcription. Since the 1980s, other musical mediums have appeared but none have come close to the volume of Rosemary's output. She baffled the experts and psychologists of her day and though she is largely forgotten or overlooked today, she remains a fascinating and enigmatic figure.

In December 2019 during the London Contemporary Music festival, the pianist Siwan Rhys performed a selection of the music that Rosemary had transcribed from Liszt, Beethoven, and Rachmaninov so perhaps she is, at last, getting some recognition in modern times having been underrated for so long.

Rosemary Brown died in London on November 16th 2001. She published three volumes of autobiography.

Unfinished Symphonies: Voices from the Beyond (1971)
Immortals at My Elbow (1974)
Look Beyond Today (1986).

Jack Spicer (1925–1965)

Jack Spicer was an American poet who was largely unknown outside the San Francisco Bay Area until after his death. He was an early gay-rights activist in the clandestine Mattachine Society and an openly gay poet at a time when homosexuality was a taboo subject.

He was born John Lester Spicer on January 30th 1925 in Los Angeles and received his early education at Fairfax High School until 1942. He attended the University of Redlands (1943–1945) and then studied linguistics and poetic history at the University of California in Berkeley (1945–1955) except for 1950–1952 when he spent nearly two years as a teacher at the University of Minnesota because he refused to sign the anti-communist loyalty oath pertaining to California at that time.

In the late 1940s, he met two other gay poets, Robert Duncan and Robin Blaser, and they formed the 'Berkeley Renaissance' creating a new form of poetry. This coterie would, in time, develop into the 'San Francisco Renaissance'.

In 1954, in conjunction with five painter friends, Spicer was a co-founder of San Francisco's Six Gallery where Allen Ginsberg (1926–1997) gave a reading of *Howl* on October 7th 1955, thus launching the West Coast Beat movement.

In a move to find greater scope for his work, Spicer moved to New York City in 1955 and then Boston, where he worked for a time in the Rare Book Room at Boston Public Library but returned to San Francisco in 1956. He then began work on his first book 'dictated' via automatic writing *After Lorca* (1957), during which time he started to receive what he termed 'poetry as dictation'. The book is a collection of poems 'received' from Federico Garcia Lorca (1898–1936), interspersed with letters to the deceased Spanish poet from Spicer, and including an introduction by Garcia Lorca himself. In the introduction, Garcia Lorca clearly states that nearly half of the poems are not his and that Spicer's collection 'may lead him to write better poetry of his own'. *After Lorca* was his first example of what he termed 'serial poetry' and this long narrative form dominated his work from then on and he wrote fewer single, stand-alone poems.

After 1957, his life became increasingly difficult and was fraught with bitterness, anger, despair, and disappointment. Some of his friends were marginalised, poorly paid jobs came and went, and he fell into alcoholism.

In June 1965, Spicer visited Vancouver and gave a series of legendary lectures explaining his ideas about the creation of poetry as a spiritual practice. He described the automatic writing sessions of WB Yeats and his wife Georgie as an example of how he received 'poetry by dictation' from what he often termed the 'Outside'. He stated that to achieve this, a poet would have to remove himself from the traditional poetic experience in order that the 'spooks' and 'Martians' could enter. Spicer often referred to Jean Cocteau's film *Orphée* (1949) and compared a poet to the car radio that receives poetry from hell. He did not believe that the poet's work was inspired from within but that external forces invaded the writer and dictated the message directly. Spicer did not advocate automatic writing per se but favoured a controlled readiness for the 'Outside' whilst filtering out personal elements such as desire, love, and self-expression. As Spicer himself stated 'I really honestly don't feel that I own my poems and I don't feel proud of them'. He once said, 'When someone praises my work I feel like they're talking about my brother'.

In August 1965, Spicer collapsed into a coma in the lift of his apartment building at Long Beach. With nothing to identify him at the time, he was admitted to the poverty ward at San Francisco General Hospital where he was visited by Robin Blaser. After days spent in a feverish and mostly incoherent state, his last words were 'My vocabulary did this to me'. His long years of alcohol abuse had finally caught up with him and he died on August 17th 1965 aged 40.

The publication of *The Collected Books of Jack Spicer* in 1975 brought him wider recognition and his writing now influences poetry throughout Europe, Canada, and the U.S.. A collection of Jack Spicer's work, *My Vocabulary Did This to Me: The Collected Poetry of Jack Spicer* (edited by Peter Gizzi and Kevin Killian) was published in 2008 and it won the American Book Award in 2009.

James Ingram Merrill (1926–1995)

Merrill was one of many authors who believed that automatic writing contributed to their work and he is best known for *The Changing Light at Sandover* (1982), the series of poems inspired by the communications received from spirit guides through the medium of a Ouija board.

James Merrill was born in New York City on March 3rd 1926. His father, Charles E Merrill (1885–1956), was a founding partner of the Merrill Lynch investment company. The family wealth enabled James to grow up in privileged circumstances and enjoy a private education. His governess Mademoiselle was fluent in several languages and she stimulated his interest in poetry. He attended St Bernard's Grammar School from 1936–1938 before becoming a boarder at Lawrenceville School, Princeton. When James was sixteen, his father secretly gathered his poems and short stories and published them as a surprise at Christmas 1942. *Jim's Book* pleased James originally but in later life he was embarrassed by it. It was printed as a limited edition of an estimated 200 copies and is now extremely rare. After Lawrenceville, James attended Amherst College, a private liberal arts college in Massachusetts. His education was disrupted by an eight-month spell in the United States Army. On his return, he was able to complete his thesis on Marcel Proust and produce a collection of poems called *The Black Swan* (1946). This was printed privately in Athens, Greece in only 100 copies in association with his Amherst professor and lover, Kimon Friar. His first commercial enterprise was the book *First Poems* (1951) which received mixed reviews. He met his long-term partner, the writer and artist David Jackson (1922–2001), at The Comedy Club in New York where Merrill's play *The Bait* was being performed. Obviously unimpressed, Arthur Miller and Dylan Thomas walked out during the show.

Prior to the death of his father in 1955, Merrill and his two half-siblings, Charles and Doris, renounced any further inheritance and the majority of Charles Merrill's estate was given to charity.

Merrill and Jackson started experimenting with a home-made Ouija board in 1955 and Merrill began to receive messages from a spirit guide named Ephraim who was said to have been a Greek Jew born in AD 8. The lyrical and mystical messages that he transcribed shaped some of his most significant poetry and it was described as being comparable to Byron, WB Yeats, and WH Auden. The first poem that made use of the spirit messages from the Ouija board was *Voices from the Other World* (1959) and he went on to become one of the outstanding poets of his generation. Over four decades, a huge number of psychic messages were transcribed and published albeit lightly reconfigured. His main work was the trilogy *The Changing*

Light at Sandover (1982), the 560-page epic that defined his career. The first volume was *The Book of Ephraim* (1976), followed by *Mirabell: Books of Number* (1978), and *Scripts for the Pageant* (1980) and each section reflected a different segment of their Ouija board. In an interview with Tom Vitale in 1991, Merrill described the project, which took five or six years to complete, as an 'intricate kind of mandala of different forces'.

James Merrill was wealthy all his life owing to a trust set up for him in his early childhood but he always hated the emphasis placed on this by critics and the media. He had an empathy for artists and writers for whom life was a struggle. Following the death of his father in 1956, he founded the Ingram Merrill Foundation as an endowment to provide grants to writers and painters, particularly those showing early promise.

During his long career, he won every major poetry award in the United States, including the 1977 Pulitzer Prize for *Divine Comedies* (1976) and the National Book Critics Circle Award for *The Changing Light at Sandover*. He also won the National Book Award for Poetry on two occasions, the Bobbitt National Prize for Poetry, and the Bollingen Prize. He also wrote short stories, a novel, essays, plays, and a memoir, *A Different Person* (1993).

James Merrill died of a heart attack related to AIDS in Tucson, Arizona on February 6th 1995. His ashes and the remains of David Jackson are buried side by side at Evergreen Cemetery in Stonington, Connecticut.

Jane Roberts 1929–1984)

Another remarkable automatic writer was Jane Roberts. Born Dorothy Jane Roberts on May 8th 1929 in Albany, New York, she suffered poor health for much of her life. At the age of nine she developed colitis and had an overactive thyroid gland by the age of 14. Her eyesight was poor and in 1940 she was consigned to a strict Catholic orphanage in New York.

In 1932, her mother Marie experienced the early stages of rheumatoid arthritis and within a year she had become partly incapacitated. When a steady decline in Marie's condition left her bedridden, Jane had no alternative but to take care of her. When her embittered mother attempted suicide for the fifth time, Jane decided to leave saying that she could no longer cope with the constant psychological abuse.

In 1945 at the age of sixteen, she started work in a discount store and was dating an old friend from her time at Saratoga Springs by the name of Walt Zeh. They married in December 1950 and she had several jobs including being a sub-editor for a Saratoga newspaper but the couple were only together for three years. In February 1954 she met the former commercial artist Robert Fabian Butts who was ten years older than herself. Eventually they left town together and Jane sued for divorce from Walt. Jane and Robert married on December 27th 1954 in Sayre, Pennsylvania.

She wrote in a wide variety of genres including fiction, non-fiction, short stories, science fiction and fantasy, poetry, and children books. Some of her fiction covered the subjects of clairvoyance and reincarnation. She was the only woman invited to the first Milford Writers Conference for science fiction writers which took place in Milford, Pennsylvania in 1956.

In 1960, Jane and Robert moved to Elmira, New York to find steady employment and she began working in an art gallery.

The couple began to accumulate a huge amount of material that Jane received as a spirit medium from someone calling himself 'Seth'. It began in September 1963. Jane said that she was about to write some poetry when 'Between one normal minute and the next, a fantastic avalanche of radical, new ideas burst into my head with tremendous force. It was as if the physical world were really tissue-paper-thin, hiding infinite dimensions of reality, and I was flung through the tissue paper with a huge ripping sound.' When she recovered, Jane discovered that she had written a collection of notes bearing the title '*The Physical Universe as Idea Construction*'. Prior to this, the couple had little belief in paranormal abilities but the event aroused their curiosity and Jane was able to get a contract with a New York publisher to write a book on extra-sensory perception. Before the end of

1963, Jane and Robert had started using a Ouija board as part of their research for the book.

On December 2nd 1963, the first messages arrived from the person they later discovered to be Seth. The early sessions were conducted using the Ouija board but on January 2nd 1964, Jane started to receive the messages in her head and dictated them to Robert whilst in a trance state. Two weeks later, Jane received a message from a woman who had recently died. She told the couple that their connection with Seth would be a lifetime's work. Seth suggested how to arrange the furniture in their home to suit their respective energies and though Jane and Robert were unsure about the messages, they agreed to the request. The first time a session was attended by anyone else was on February 18th 1964 and the following evening, they gave up the use of the Ouija board altogether.

Jane thought that Seth was a fantasy that she had unwittingly summoned from her subconscious because, at that time, she did not believe in life after death. Concerned about her mental well-being, she consulted a psychologist but ceased worrying about her situation when she came to the conclusion that of the two of them, Seth was more mature and well-balanced than the psychologist.

Jane also employed a typewriter to produce automatic writing and claimed to receive messages from the artists Rembrandt (1606–1669) and Paul Cézanne (1839–1906), and also from among others, the American philosopher William James (1842–1910).

For the last 21 years of her life, Jane held more than 1,500 sessions channelling information from Seth and these were often attended by witnesses. For a few years, Jane hosted weekly Extra Sensory Perception classes in her home and she often received messages from Seth that would be shared with her students. Although she only charged attendees two or three dollars per session, even these modest fees were dropped when her books began to sell in appreciable numbers. Many people wrote to her asking for help and the sessions that she gave them were always free of charge. The published manuscripts were known as the Seth Material and they established Jane as a prominent figure in the world of paranormal phenomena. Jane never claimed to be the author except for her role as medium in channelling the texts although some of her own poetry was occasionally included to illustrate how her own writing was influenced by Seth's concepts. In total, *The Seth Material* ran to ten volumes but Jane's advancing illness meant that the last two volumes appeared to be incomplete. Robert Butts' extensive contributions to the Seth books in terms of appendices and footnotes meant that he was co-author of them. Jane described Seth as an 'energy personality essence no longer focused in physical matter'. When dictating Seth's messages, her voice became deeper and had a distinct but unidentifiable accent.

Jane also wrote *The Oversoul Seven* trilogy, a fictional work that looked at Seth's teachings on the topics of reincarnation and oversouls.

At the beginning of 1982, Jane was hospitalised with multiple symptoms, including her continuing thyroid problems, severe hearing loss, double vision, anaemia, and various infections. She partially recovered but died two and a half years later in Elmira, Chemung County, New York on September 5th 1984. She was bedridden for the last 18 months of her life by the rheumatoid arthritis that had plagued her for many years. Jane was just 55 years old when she died and Robert Butts continued to manage the Seth texts and oversee the publication of any remaining material. Robert ensured that all the manuscripts, notes, and recordings were left to the Yale University Library. The archive entitled 'Jane Roberts Papers' is held in 498 boxes and occupies 164 feet of shelf space.

He remarried and his second wife helped him to continue the work until his death from cancer on May 26th 2008.

Jane Roberts Butts and Robert Fabian Butts are buried together in the Furnaceville cemetery in Wayne County, New York.

Her books have sold nearly eight million copies in more than a dozen languages although naturally not without a certain amount of criticism. The poet Charles Upton, in his book *The System of Antichrist* (2001), suggested that Jane Roberts multiplied the self due to a fear of death. Other opinions speculated on the possibility of fraud or that everything had sprung from the subconscious. A few religious groups gave the usual warnings regarding the dangers of channelled messaging and there were the typical voices of dissent from the syndicated religious programmes that litter American television networks. Some of Jane's work was criticised as having a misunderstanding of both Christian and Eastern philosophy but this did not prevent Deepak Chopra and Louise May from stating that the material had had a profound influence on their thinking. Whatever one makes of Jane's life and work, there can be no argument that she made an indelible mark on the world of the paranormal.

Matthew Manning (1955–)

Matthew Manning has had a remarkable life. Automatic writing and drawing have been just two of his many powerful, paranormal experiences. He was born in Redruth, Cornwall on August 17th 1955 and at the age of eleven, he and his family experienced intense poltergeist activity at their modern house in Shelford near Cambridge. For several months, their lives were disrupted by repeated knocking and the unexplained movement of dozens of articles. The phenomenon subsided and the family moved to an 18th century house in Linton about eight miles away. Within a short period of time and with Matthew now 15, the poltergeist returned with an increased ferocity. Wardrobe doors opened and closed, furniture was found piled up, and ornaments and things continued to be moved around. On occasion, his bed would vibrate and rise off the floor and his brother and sister who were younger were frightened by large objects such as a trolley floating in the air. Apports (objects appearing from an unknown source) appeared in the house and the items included fossils, beads, an old candle, and an ancient loaf of bread. His spirit guide during this time was a man named Thomas Penn who, upon receiving a person's date of birth from Matthew, was able to provide an accurate medical diagnosis.

Matthew attended Oakham School in Rutland as a boarder whereupon the poltergeist followed him and its activities were witnessed by 24 pupils in his dormitory. Heavy beds moved around, water appeared on the floor, and stones, cutlery, and dinner plates appeared as if out of nowhere. The activity only lessened when Matthew started to receive automatic writing and this arrived in English, German, Italian, Russian, Arabic, Latin and Greek. One day at school, he was working on an essay but without much success. He was wondering what to write when, quite suddenly, his hand was drawn to the paper and he started to write garbled sentences in an unfamiliar handwriting, even when in the company of six school friends. After this episode, poltergeist activity ceased for more than 36 hours. Another paranormal experience occurred at the school when he was able to use astral projection to 'visit' his home and see the inside of the house.

On July 31st 1971, the walls and ceiling of Matthew's bedroom began to accumulate hundreds of roughly written signatures of deceased people. The inscriptions continued for a week even when the house was deliberately unoccupied. Before being painted over, they were photographed and many of the names appeared in local parish registers and some bore dates that covered six centuries. The first one to arrive was signed 'Robert Webbe' who dated from the 17th century. The name 'Webbe' frequently appeared and some members of the family had been former tenants of the house whilst others lived in the vicinity. Matthew received a lot of automatic writing from Robert Webbe that contained confusing dates but this was resolved when he discovered that he was dealing with two people of that name, one who had died in 1713 and one who had built the front of their house in 1731.

Like Rosemary Brown, Matthew had multiple automatism abilities. His mother suggested that he try automatic drawing, arguing that if he were to produce work far in excess of his own artistic skills, then the results would be proven to have originated independently from Matthew. The results were startling and without going into a trance, he produced works of high quality that appeared to be by Pablo Picasso, Aubrey Beardsley, Paul Klee, Henri Matisse, Albrecht Dürer, Leonardo da Vinci, and Francisco Goya. Some of the drawings were copies of known works but some of them were 'new' or unknown and many were signed with an apparently authentic signature. Each one began in the centre of the page and was produced in one to two hours, a fraction of the time that the living artist would have needed. Matthew accepted that 80% of the drawings probably arose from his subconscious but said that he had no explanation for the source of the remaining 20%.

During a session of automatic writing in April 1972, Matthew received a message from Frederick W Myers who was one of the founders of the Society for Psychical Research. Although encouraging in nature, it warned Matthew about the dangers of automatic writing and the difficulty of convincing others of its validity.

His plans to attend Sussex University and study psychology were set aside in order that he could write a book about his experiences. *The Link: Extraordinary Gifts of a Teenage Psychic* (1974) described his psychic experiences, medical diagnoses, metal bending, and his collaborative work with leading scientists. The book, which ran to nineteen editions and was translated into sixteen languages, also included the investigations and support he received from George Owen of the Cambridge Psychical Research Society. A friend of his publisher took him to Claridge's to meet David Frost who immediately offered Matthew a whole episode of *The Frost Interview* to explain and demonstrate his abilities to a huge audience. The show made him a household name and led to a tour of the United States where his appearances on television helped to make *The Link* a best seller. Frost became an advocate of Matthew's work and other American tours followed as did trips to Japan and Spain. Frost was of the opinion that the closer science got to developing technology that was capable of understanding and measuring Matthew's psychic encounters, the more the world would be ready to recognise the legitimacy of those events. The pair remained friends until Frost's death on August 31st 2013.

Of his second book, *In the Minds of Millions* (1974), Matthew said it 'Is intended to be a record of the experiences shared with scientists, journalists, and people in the public eye – events the veracity of which can be corroborated by those scientists and journalists and individuals'.

His ability as a clairvoyant was demonstrated in June 1975 when, nearly a week before it occurred, he predicted the Eastern Airlines plane crash at John F Kennedy airport in New York in which 113 passengers and crew lost their lives. He was also known for the effect that his presence could have on electrical equipment which could break down without warning. This was a common occurrence and had caused disruption during the recording of *The Frost Report*. Owing to this tendency, Matthew always booked airline seats that were well away from the flight deck.

Over the years, skeptics have persistently doubted the authenticity of the paranormal incidents surrounding his life but their opinions must be set against the many witnesses and trained observers who had first-hand experience of these astonishing events. At one time, the security services interviewed him about the possibility of his abilities being harnessed to assist the nation although some factions considered him to be a security risk.

In 1976, he questioned his having to endure the relentless rounds of media exposure and early in 1977 retreated to Shimla and Narkand in India to spend some time in the foothills of the Himalayas. From that point on, he was only involved in research that might be of help to other people and spent five years demonstrating his psychic healing ability at the University of London, the Mind Science Foundation in Texas, and at the UCLA.

Towards the end of 1977, Matthew distanced himself from the word 'psychic' and declared that he wished to be described as a 'mentalist'.

He has given talks on healing to prestigious gatherings including a Buckingham House dinner in July 1979 on the theme of 'Supernature', the Royal Society of Medicine in 1986, and the Parliamentary Group for Alternative and Complementary Medicine at the Houses of Parliament on October 28th 1997. He has given consultations to many famous people including Prince Philip, John Cleese, Van Morrison, Brian Clough, and many others including professional sports personalities and familiar names from the entertainment world. In spite of his worldwide recognition and reputation, Matthew has never exploited this in pursuit of great wealth.

During his life, he had regularly invited and undertaken scientific and medical examination in the U.K. and the U.S. but by 1982, he had become disillusioned by the hundreds of laboratory tests. He decided to devote his time and spiritual energy to healing and giving lectures and it is in that realm that he may be found today.

Automatism in Art

In physiology, automatism describes spontaneous and automatic movements of the body such as breathing or sleepwalking.

In art terms, automatism usually refers to a method of subconscious drawing in which the artist accesses material from the unconscious mind and removes conscious thought from the creative process.

Automatic drawing has a long history in Spiritualism and the psychic arts but it was the Dadaists and Surrealists who popularised the method of releasing the creative power of the unconscious in art. Through such methods as free association and collage, they saw it as a means to escape from the straitjacket of historical values and intellectual constraints. However, not all surrealist works were the product of automatism and the automatic drawings often involved conscious intervention to achieve a more recognisable image. However, the Surrealists' use of automatism helped in the development of Art Informel which encompassed a myriad of approaches to abstract art in the 1940s and 1950s. Improvisation and gestural art were central to Art Informel and it spread across Europe at a time when Abstract Expressionism and Action Painting were gaining prominence in the United States.

In the 1940s, Les Automatistes further cemented the role of automatism in art. Prior to these movements, primitive forms of automatism could be found in the work of Alexander Cozens (1717–1786) whose landscapes were sometimes created from abstract blots of paint on paper. The English painter and printmaker William Blake (1757–1827) claimed that the spirit of his younger brother Robert, who died of tuberculosis aged 24, guided some of his illustrations and also showed him a new technique for printing his works, which Blake called 'illuminated printing'.

The boundaries of automatism were blurred further by artists such as Andy Warhol (1928–1987) who produced artwork under the influence of drugs.

Many prominent artists experimented with automatism and the following pages include some that are worthy of inclusion. This is an illustrative list rather than an exhaustive one. The reader may feel that a particular artist is not included or too thinly covered but one of the aims of this book is to encourage people to do their own research and further their knowledge of what interests them.

Hilma af Klint (1862–1944)

Hilma af Klint was born at the Karlberg Palace military academy in Stockholm on October 26th 1862. She was one of Europe's first abstract painters although she was largely unknown outside Stockholm in her lifetime. She studied at what is now Konstfack University before gaining admission to the Royal Academy of Fine Arts in Stockholm in 1882. Following her graduation in 1887, one of the first women to do so, she gained recognition for her conventional drawings, portraits, and landscapes. She worked briefly as a draughtsperson for a veterinary institute where she produced detailed drawings of animal surgery. Her interest in the natural world never left her and she created numerous botanical works.

She attended her first Spiritist meetings and séances in 1879 and when her sister Hermina died in 1880, this intensified her interest in the spiritual side of her life. She was influenced by Madame Blavatsky and the Theosophical Society, becoming a member in 1889. She was also interested in the philosophy of the Rosicrucians. To Hilma, reality was not confined to the physical world but included the inner realm of spirit.

Along with her close friend Anna Cassel (who she had met at the Academy), Sigrid Hedman, Cornelia Cederberg, and Mathilda Nilsson, she became a member of the Edelweiss Society in 1896. The society incorporated a combination of Spiritualism and Theosophy and these women went on to form 'The Friday Group' now known as 'The Five', an association of like-minded artists. They were all fascinated by the paranormal and regularly held séances, where they received messages from 'The High Ones' also known as 'The High Masters', which were recorded in notebooks. Through her association with 'The Five', Hilma af Klint began to create automatic drawing in 1896. She felt that her hand was being guided by an external influence and wrote 'The pictures were painted directly through me, without any preliminary drawings, and with great force. I had no idea what the paintings were supposed to depict; nevertheless I worked swiftly and surely, without changing a single brush stroke'. Hilma did not see herself as just a medium that her spirit masters could control. She wrote 'It was not the case that I was to blindly obey the spirits, but that I was to imagine that they were always standing by my side'. The resulting paintings were often of a geometric nature and were a graphical depiction of mystical concepts and visualisations of the astral world. In 1905, aged 43 and after ten years of study, her spirit guide 'Amaliel' gave her the task of creating the 'Paintings for the Temple' although she never knew to what this referred.

They were created during the periods 1906–1908 and 1912–1915 and comprised 193 paintings. This included the 1907 series known as 'The Ten Largest' and each painting measures approximately 240cm x 320cm. Soon after she had completed the 'Paintings for The Temple', her divine guidance came to an end and she felt free to pursue her own direction in abstract art and from 1922 she began to use watercolours in addition to oils. The abstract paintings that she created from 1906 onwards were radically different from what had gone before in the art world. Her work pre-dated Mondrian and Kandinsky and though her contemporaries exhibited extensively, she made limited efforts to show her own work in public, keeping most of it private. Except for one notable exception. In July 1928, the World Conference on Spiritual Science took place in London. Although originally excluded, Hilma af Klint travelled by sea to London along with some of her large-scale paintings. In spite of there being no list of works, it seems fairly certain that some works from the 'Paintings for the Temple' series were on show.

In 1908 she met Rudolf Steiner for the first time and he accepted her invitation to see the first series of the 'Paintings for the Temple'. Steiner saw the 111 paintings but left largely unimpressed by the work, stating that her methods were incompatible with Theosophy. During his visit to her studio, Steiner insisted that Hilma's contemporaries would not understand the paintings and that 50 years would have to pass before they could be interpreted. He did pay close attention to the 'Primordial Chaos group' but the damage had been done. Distressed at his reaction to her work and with the added responsibility of having to care for her mother who was frail and blind, it seems clear that she ceased painting for four years. Steiner founded the Anthroposophical Society in 1913 and in 1920, she met him again at the society's headquarters at the Goetheanum in Dornach, Switzerland. In the same year, she joined the society and over the next ten years spent long periods at the Goetheanum. Anthroposophy is a form of spiritual philosophy which supports the concept that human experience is informed by another world that deals with our spiritual and artistic needs.

Following her death in 1944, her will instructed that her work, 1,200 paintings, 125 diaries, and 26,000 pages of notes, should not be shown for a period of 20 years. This was partly due to the 'High Ones' who, many years earlier, had instructed her not to show the paintings to anyone. Also, it was her belief that her works would only be understood in the future.

Hilma left her work in the care of her nephew Erik af Klint who subsequently offered her works to Stockholm's Moderna Museet (Museum of Modern Art). They rejected the collection when the museum's director discovered that she had been a medium and a mystic. Erik then donated her works to the Hilma af Klint Foundation in Stockholm in the 1970s. This safeguarded Hilma's paintings and enabled them to be kept together for ever.

Her work was not widely shown in public until 1986–1987, at 'The Spiritual in Art, Abstract Painting 1890–1985' exhibition held at the Los Angeles County Museum of Art. The exhibition then moved on to Chicago and The Hague. It would be 2013 before she achieved full international recognition through the 'Pioneer of Abstraction' exhibition held at the Moderna Museet in Stockholm. Featuring 230 paintings, the exhibition travelled across Europe and was seen by more than a million people. In 2018–2019, her paintings were displayed at the Guggenheim Museum in New York and the retrospective 'Hilma af Klint: Paintings for the Future' was seen by 600,000 visitors which broke all attendance records.

Curiously, among her last paintings, there are two watercolours from 1932 predicting the events of World War II, titled *The Blitz over London* and *The Mediterranean Naval Battle*.

She died aged 81 in Djursholm, Sweden on October 21st 1944, following a traffic accident. She is buried at Galärvarvskyrkogården in Stockholm.

Wassily Kandinsky (1866–1944)

Wassily Kandinsky was a Russian painter and art theorist. He was a pioneer of abstract art although he was pre-dated by Hilma af Klint whose first abstract painting was created in Stockholm in 1906.

He was born on December 16th 1866 in Moscow. At age five, the family moved to Odessa where he attended grammar school and learned to play the cello and piano. He graduated at Grekov Odessa Art school before acceding to his parents' wishes by studying law and economics at Moscow University in 1886. Six years later in 1892, he married his cousin, Anna Chimyakina.

In 1896, he was appointed a Professor of Law at the Derpt University in Tartu but abandoned a successful career at the age of thirty to devote his life to painting. He left Tartu and travelled to Munich where he entered Anton Azbe's private painting school. However, he rapidly outgrew the school and joined the Munich Academy of Arts where he studied under Franz Stuck.

In 1901, he founded the art group Phalanx in Munich and started his own art school.

In 1902, Kandinsky encouraged Gabriela Münter (1877–1962) to enrol at his painting classes near Munich. Their intimate relationship led Kandinsky to divorce Anna. One of his most important paintings from the 1900s was *The Blue Rider* (1903).

The next few years saw Wassily and Gabriela travelling across Europe and taking part in exhibitions. Upon their return to Germany, they settled down in Murnau, a small town at the edge of the Bavarian Alps where Kandinsky chiefly painted landscapes and towns although they were mostly devoid of any human figures. He also created images based on Russian folk art at this time.

An early influence was Richard Wagner's *Lohengrin*. He was also spiritually influenced by Madame Blavatsky (1831–1891) and the Theosophical Society which he joined in 1909 having read *Thought-Forms* (1901) by Annie Besant and Charles Leadbeater.

In 1909, he co-founded The Munich New Artists Association (Neue Künstlervereinigung) in Munich and when the group dissolved in 1911, Kandinsky, together with Frans Marc, established the group called 'The Blue Rider' (Der Blaue Reiter), a group of German abstract expressionists that included Albert Bloch and Paul Klee.

Some of his paintings were titled 'Compositions' which referred to a painting with a pre-conceived composition and some 'Improvisations' meaning that the painting had no pre-conceived limitations. Kandinsky's text *Über das Geistige in der Kunst* (1911) defined impressions as being based on external reality whereas improvisations and compositions depicted images drawn from the unconscious, a state that closely relates to the automatism of the Surrealists and his exploration of spirituality in art. Like Jackson Pollock, many of his works were untitled to distance both himself and the viewer from any pre-knowledge of the content.

Kandinsky was forced to leave Germany at the start of World War 1 and he and Gabriela moved to Switzerland on August 3rd 1914. By November of that year they had separated and Kandinsky travelled to Moscow. Whilst there, he met Nina Andreevskaya (1899–1980), the daughter of a Russian General, and they were married on February 11th 1917.

From 1918 until 1921, he cooperated with the People's Committee of Education in the field of art training and museum reform. He helped in the founding of 22 provincial museums but his curriculum based on the analysis of form and colour drew such heavy criticism from his colleagues that he and Nina decided to leave Moscow in December 1921 and move to Germany.

The founder of Bauhaus, Walter Gropius, invited him to teach at the Bauhaus school of art and architecture at Weimar in 1922. Right wing hostility pushed Bauhaus to Dessau and then Berlin until the Nazis closed it in 1933. He also lectured and exhibited in the United States in 1924 as one of Die Blaue Vier (The Blue Four) and produced his legendary stage design for Mussorgsky's *Pictures at an Exhibition* in 1928 at Dessau. Between 1926 and 1933, Kandinsky painted 159 oils and 300 watercolours. Unfortunately, the Nazis declared Kandinsky's paintings to be 'degenerate' and many of them have been lost. Other works were lost during British air raids in World War 2. He and Nina emigrated to France, where he lived for the rest of his life. In 1939, he became a French citizen and created some of his most outstanding works of art. The Parisian art scene did not readily accept abstract painting and Kandinsky led a fairly lonely life, being separated from his old friends and colleagues. In spite of this, the final regeneration of his painting methods occurred. Largely avoiding the use of primary colours, he worked with soft and subtle shades. Biomorphic elements, which for so long had been absent, appeared in his pictures as if they were floating across the canvas. Kandinsky described this period to be 'really a picturesque fairy tale'.

He died in Neuilly-sur-Seine, Paris on December 13th 1944 three days before his 78th birthday.

In June 2017, *Painting with White Lines* (1913) sold at Sotheby's in London for £33 million.

Pablo Picasso (1881–1973)

Picasso was a Spanish painter, sculptor, printmaker, ceramicist and theatre designer. He was born on October 25th 1881 in Málaga, Spain. One of the most influential artists of the 20th century, he is known for co-founding the Cubist movement with Georges Braque and for the wide variety of styles that he helped develop. Among his most famous works are the proto-Cubist *Les Demoiselles d'Avignon* (1907) and *Guernica* (1937).

Picasso exhibited Cubist works at the first Surrealist group exhibition in 1925 but the Surrealists' concept of 'psychic automatism in its pure state' never fully appealed to him. However, he seemed to have introduced a type of automatic drawing in his etchings and lithographs of the 1960s.

The harlequin became a personal motif for Picasso although this was later replaced by the Minotaur which was commonly used by the Surrealists.

He wrote over 300 poems and two full-length plays, *Desire Caught by the Tail* (1941), and *The Four Little Girls* (1949).

Picasso used common house paint in many of his paintings which were painted mostly from imagination or memory.

He died on April 8th 1973 in Mougins, France. His wife Jacqueline never came to terms with his death and committed suicide in 1986, aged just 59.

Picasso was more prolific than most artists of his era and the only one to rival his output is the American artist Bob Ross.

Interestingly, more of Picasso's paintings have been stolen than those of any other artist.

Madge Gill (1882–1961)

Another fascinating automatist was Madge Gill who was born in London on January 19th 1882. She overcame the early traumas of being sent to a Barnardo's orphanage (while her mother was still alive) and being sent to Canada under a child labour scheme until she was able to return to the U.K. in 1900. On March 3rd 1920, aged 38, Madge Gill saw a vision in the sky of Jesus surrounded by angels. This was the catalyst for Madge's possession by her spirit guide Myrninerest, under whose influence she began to prolifically draw, paint, write, and sew in spite of the recent loss of an eye. Like other Spiritualists, Madge insisted that she was merely a conduit through which Myrninerest could communicate and took no credit for the art she created. They would maintain contact until Madge died and the thousands of enigmatic drawings that they created are among the most remarkable examples of mediumistic art. Primarily in pen and ink, her 'guided' drawings ranged in size from postcard to rolls of calico cloth many yards in width. Her work is considered to fall under 'Outsider Art', the term coined by the art historian Roger Cardinal (1940–2019) in his book 'Outsider Art' (1972). She experimented with a variety of media including writing, knitting, weaving, and crochet work. Madge died in London on January 28th 1961 and in recent years, her work has become of increasing interest.

Jean Arp (1886–1966)

Jean Arp was born Hans Peter Wilhelm Arp on September 16th 1886 in Strasbourg (then part of Germany). When Alsace was returned to France at the end of World War I, French law determined that he be known as 'Jean' although he continued to call himself 'Hans' when he spoke German. He was a painter, sculptor, and poet and experimented widely with automatic drawing. He was a founder member of the Dada movement, a pioneer of abstract art, and one of the leaders of the European avant-garde movement.

From 1904–1907, he studied at the École des Arts et Métiers in Strasbourg before attending the Kunstschule in Weimar, Germany. In 1908, he studied at the Académie Julian in Paris. From 1909, he travelled widely in Europe, becoming acquainted with Picasso, Kandinsky, Modigliani, and others.

In 1911, he co-founded and exhibited with Der Moderne Bund, an organisation in Lucerne that encouraged the acceptance of Modernism in Switzerland. In 1912, he moved to Munich where Kandinski encouraged his involvement with the German Expressionist group, Der Blaue Reiter.

He was in Paris at the onset of World War 1 and was forced to seek refuge in Zurich in neutral Switzerland where he feigned mental illness to avoid military service. It was here that Arp became associated with Richard Huelsenbeck, Hugo Ball, and Tristan Tzara and they founded the Dada movement and the Cabaret Voltaire in Zurich. During this period he met Sophie Taeuber, the Swiss artist who became his first wife on October 20th 1922. Towards the end of World War 1, Arp moved away from regular geometric forms. He created free flowing work in the absence of deliberate conscious actions akin to the methods employed by André Masson. He was one of the first artists to employ chance and randomness to create works of art and produced a series of automatic drawings where he relinquished control and allowed the pen or pencil to meander at random. This method would later influence Jackson Pollock and the Abstract Expressionists.

Although he remained loyal to Dada, he co-founded the Surrealist movement in Paris in the mid-1920s. He exhibited with the group at the Galerie Pierre in Paris where his work appeared alongside that of Paul Klee, Man Ray, Max Ernst, Joan Miró, and André Masson. A few years later, Arp had his first solo exhibition at the Galerie Surréaliste in Paris, took French citizenship, and went to live in Clamart in south west Paris. It was in Paris that he established the automatic writing and drawing techniques that would influence the future development of Abstract Expressionism and his writing was widely published in magazines such as *La Révolution surréaliste*. Arp's work in the 1920s was dominated by painted wooden bas-reliefs that he sawed into unusual shapes that were inspired by structures found in nature.

From the 1930s onwards, Arp wrote and published poetry and essays. He and Sophie also collaborated on collages and tapestries including Arp's 'chance collages' which he termed Papiers Dechirés (Torn Papers) whereby he allowed scraps of paper to fall freely on to a large paper sheet, glueing them in the position where they had landed.

The 1930s saw Arp create his most famous works, the biomorphic sculptures. Using materials such as bronze, marble, and plaster, they were to dominate his art for decades. He later wrote 'I only have to move my hands... The forms that then take shape offer access to mysteries and reveal to us the profound sources of life.' The freestanding sculptures did not depict a theme and Arp only gave titles to his works after he had finished them. He did not view such work as abstract art and along with other artists referred to it as Concrete Art. He became a member of Cercle et Carré and Abstraction Création, the French artists' groups that promoted Concrete Art.

When Paris fell to the Germans in 1942, Arp left Paris for Zurich where he remained, only returning to Clamart in Paris in 1946. In 1943, Sophie tragically died from carbon monoxide poisoning caused by a faulty stove at a friend's house in Zurich. He withdrew from the public gaze and fell into a deep depression for several years, which stopped his creative work, and he found comfort through studying mystical Christian and Tibetan texts.

Marguerite Hagenbach (1902–1994), who had been dealing with his administration, joined him on his first trip to America in 1949 where he had a solo exhibition at Curt Valentin's Buchholz Gallery in New York. Although they were already a couple, they would not marry until 1959 when Arp's failing health prevented him from travelling and they bought a property in Locarno, Switzerland, which is still owned by the Arp Foundation.

In 1950, Arp was commissioned by the architect Walter Gropius to create a large-scale relief sculpture in wood for the Graduate Center at Harvard University in Massachusetts. Soon after, Arp completed his first monumental sculpture *Cloud Shepherd* for the University of Caracas in Venezuela.

He received a multitude of awards during his career, including the 1954 Grand Prize for Sculpture at the Venice Biennale and was made a Chevalier of the French Legion of Honour in 1960. His busy final years received much recognition, including major retrospectives at the Museum of Modern Art in New York in 1958 and at the Musée National d'Art Moderne, Paris in 1962.

Jean Arp died, following a heart attack, on June 7th 1966, in Basel, Switzerland at the age of 79. His work hangs in museums around the world and there is a large collection at the Museum of Modern and Contemporary Art in Strasbourg.

Austin Osman Spare (1886–1956)

It is quite likely that you have never heard of Austin Osman Spare but he should have been a famous artist and illustrator and at least as well-known as Aubrey Beardsley. He was born in the Bloomfield House tenement in Snow Hill, London on December 30th 1886 and attended the local St Sepulchre Church School and then the St Agnes Church School in Kennington. He took an early interest in art and at the age of twelve, attended evening classes at Lambeth School of Art. Whilst working at Powell's glassworks, which had links to William Morris and the Arts and Crafts movement, his drawings were spotted by Sir William Blake Richmond and FH Richmond. They recommended him for a scholarship to the Royal College of Art in South Kensington and he was the youngest entrant at the 1904 Royal Academy summer exhibition. His drawings were also on show at the Paris International Exhibition and the St Louis Exposition. Whilst at the RCA, he developed a strong friendship with the suffragette Sylvia Pankhurst but he left the college in 1905 without any qualifications. Having left the RCA, he became a bookplate designer and illustrator, published his first political cartoon, and illustrated a second publication *A Book of Satyrs* which consisted of a series of nine images satirising the establishment. The property developer Pickford Waller was Spare's main patron during this period but he also became popular among avant-garde society in Edwardian London and several known homosexuals also became patrons of his work.

From his teens, Spare developed his own religious philosophy which is now known as the Zos Kia Cultus. The term was coined by the occultist Kenneth Grant following Spare's need to devise a religion of his own which embodied his conception of what we are, we were, and shall be in the future. Spare had a strong interest in Theosophy and read several books by Madame Blavatsky. His fascination with Occultism led him to write and illustrate *Earth Inferno* (1905), the first of his three grimoires that also included *The Book of Pleasure* (1913) and *The Focus of Life* (1921).

He developed automatic writing and automatic drawing some years before the Surrealists, and what he termed sigilization where sigils were employed to create entities from the subconscious rather than the traditional medieval concept of using them to invoke elemental forces. Symbolism and Art Nouveau were strong influences for Spare and his occult artworks often featured grotesque or sexual imagery.

For a while, he was involved with Aleister Crowley and his A∴A∴ or Argenteum Astrum which Crowley had co-founded in 1907. Spare believed in Thelema, an occult religion that Crowley had set up in 1904 and submitted drawings to the organisation's journal *The Equinox*. Spare left the A∴A∴ in 1912, objecting to its hierarchical structure and ceremonial magic.

Spare fell in love with the actress Eily Gertrude Shaw (1888–1938) and she posed for a number of portraits before their marriage on September 4th 1911. They moved into a flat in Golders Green before moving later to a flat in Kennington. However, the relationship was a difficult one and she was described as being 'unintellectual and materialistic'. By the beginning of World War 1, financial problems and his sexual reputation, along with his fourth book *The Focus of Life* (1921) which contained voluptuous pencil nudes proved enough to bring about the end of the marriage. By 1919, they had separated and Spare moved to Bloomsbury although they remained married.

The years between 1909 and 1913 were Spare's most productive period. He held many London exhibitions and enjoyed many commissions from publishers and collectors. Spare's masterpiece *The Book of Pleasure: The Psychology of Ecstasy* (1913), which was inspired by his marriage to Eily, is regarded as a classic in esoteric studies. In the book, Spare refers to automatic writing, saying that it allowed the unconscious mind to produce works of art and automatism came to form the basis of the artist's method of working. He believed that the unconscious part of the mind was the only source of inspiration. In spite of his interest in the unconscious, Spare gave no credence to the ideas proposed by Sigmund Freud and Carl Jung, referring to them as 'Fraud and Junk.'

Declared unfit for active service, he worked as an official war artist in World War 1 during which period he briefly published the art magazines *Form* and *The Golden Hind*. After the war, he fell into poverty but continued to exhibit his work.

Class distinction and a scant education proved to be stumbling blocks to commercial success and his career struggled in the early 1920s by which time he was living in a Southwark council flat. He became a recluse and devoted himself to automatic and psychic drawing. In 1924, Spare produced a sketchbook of automatic drawings titled *The Book of Ugly Ecstasy* which contained a collection of grotesque creatures. In 1925, he produced a similar publication titled *A Book of Automatic Drawings*. This was followed by a further set of pictures titled *The Valley of Fear*. His last published book was another piece of automatic writing titled *Anathema of Zos: The Sermon to the Hypocrites* (1927). It was not well received but after his 1927 and 1929 shows failed, he produced his most successful work for years. His exhibition at the Godfrey Philips Gallery in November 1930 'Experiments in Reality' was full of beautiful anamorphic portraits of film stars and young women, including Jean Harlow and Mary Pickford.

Interest in his work was revived by the arrival of Surrealism in London in 1936 and he was feted as having been a pioneer of the movement. Taking advantage of the new craze for Surrealism, Spare produced his Surrealist Racing Forecast Cards for use in divination, selling them by means of a small ad in *Exchange & Mart*. At the age of fifty, Spare's ability to produce fine drawings was deteriorating and he adopted the medium of pastels. His three shows of 1936, 1937, and 1938 received significant press coverage but in an air raid on May 10th 1941, his studio received a direct hit and was completely destroyed along with a couple of hundred pictures. Spare was injured in the blast and was homeless for a few months until his childhood sweetheart Ada Millicent Pain gave him a home in her basement flat in Brixton. Aged sixty and in poor health, Spare was about to enter one of the most successful periods of his life.

In November 1947, he produced more than 200 works for the sell-out show at the Archer gallery that heralded his amazing post-war renaissance. The show demonstrated Spare's increasing affinity with Spiritualism and included portraits of prominent spiritualists such as Arthur Conan Doyle. He also included a number of portraits of film stars in the exhibition, leading to them being hailed as the first examples of Pop Art in Britain. His exhibitions and shows in the early 1950s revealed a mature artist of incredible vitality and imagination. At the age of 68, his work using pastels was of the highest quality and he received the patronage of many professional people.

In 1949, Spare met Steffi and Kenneth Grant (1924–2011), a former disciple of Aleister Crowley. The Grants influenced Spare to write the occult manuscripts *The Logomachy of Zos* and *The Zoetic Grimoire of Zos*. Spare became interested in witchcraft, producing artworks with titles such as *Witchery*, *Walpurgis Vampire*, and *Satiated Succubi*. They remained great friends until Spare's death in 1956 and Grant was instrumental in maintaining Spare's legacy although his tendency to reinvent him as a dark sorcerer has misled people who are only now discovering his life and work. In later life, Grant made a variety of spurious claims regarding Spare that have been widely considered to be dubious.

Public awareness of Spare seems to have declined somewhat in the 1960s until the British art nouveau revival encouraged the slow but steady revival of interest in his work beginning in the mid-1970s.

Spare's friends frequently made mention of his kindness. He was an animal lover and cared for a multitude of stray cats that proliferated in the post war ruins of London. He was a member of the RSPCA and in many photographs he can be seen wearing his RSPCA badge.

Austin Osman Spare was still exhibiting his work up until his death in London on May 15th 1956. He was buried at St Mary's Church in Ilford. He died in obscurity but since then he has had a cult following and his art is finally gaining in popularity. The recognition that eluded him in his lifetime appears to be coming at last.

In 2016, a new street was named after him near his old home in Elephant and Castle. Spare Street, created from five refurbished and glazed fronted railway arches, is home to the local arts organisation Hotel Elephant.

Max Ernst (1891–1976)

Max Ernst was born on April 2nd 1891 in Brühl, Germany. He was a painter and sculptor and was a close friend of Jean Arp for more than fifty years. Ernst embraced the irrational and otherworldly and was attracted by the alternative reality offered by dreams and hypnosis. His work helped to inspire the development of Abstract Expressionism.

Compelled to constant re-invention, from 1919 Ernst began exploring what he called 'au-delá de la peinture' (beyond painting). His early exploration of this involved collage, a technique used by his fellow Dada artists and he and several colleagues founded the Cologne Dada group. He moved to Paris in 1922 and in 1924 became an original member of the Surrealists. He developed several automatist techniques and in 1925, he started using the technique of frottage (pencil rubbings of textured surfaces) and pioneered decalcomania, the technique of pressing paint between two surfaces, producing accidental patterns and textures.

With help from Joan Miró, he developed the method of grattage where an object is placed under a piece of paper which is covered with a layer of pigment. This is scraped away to reveal an imprint of the object.

Although automatic drawing was of only minor interest to Ernst, in the mid-1940s he experimented with what he termed 'oscillation', which involved puncturing a hole in a can of paint and swinging it around to create random patterns. This technique was influential in the development of 'action painting'. He died in Paris on April 1st 1976.

Joan Miró (1893–1983)

Joan Miró was a Spanish painter, sculptor and ceramicist who embraced the automatic practice of the Surrealists. Miró has been a significant influence on late 20th-century art.

He was born on April 20th 1893 in Barcelona and attended drawing classes at the age of seven. In 1907, he enrolled at the La Llotja fine art academy before studying at the Cercle Artístic de Sant Lluc. As a teenager, he had attended business school until a bout of typhoid fever or a possible nervous breakdown in 1912 caused him to devote his life to art. He experienced many periods of depression throughout his life.

Miró was influenced by Cubism and inspired by Cézanne and van Gogh and at the age of 25, the art dealer Josep Dalmau put on his first solo show but his work was derided and vandalised. From 1920, he began to divide his time between Paris and Catalonia and his early works *Catalan Landscape* and *The Tilled Field* were among the first to be considered as surrealist, employing the symbolism that was to mark his career. When in Paris, Miró became involved with avant-garde figures including André Breton, who was interested in using art to reveal the secrets of the unconscious. Abstracted pictorial signs became a dominant feature of Miró's work in the mid-1920s and he developed a symbolic sign language which would feature in his paintings throughout the rest of his career.

Miró joined the Surrealists group in 1924. The symbolic and contradictory nature of his painting complemented the automatic techniques practised by the group and the work he created during this period came to be regarded as his 'dream paintings'. *Painting* is one of a series of works he created between 1924 and 1927 and these are frequently described as automatic paintings. His automatism and biomorphic figures intertwined to become one of Surrealism's dominant modes of painting, influencing contemporary painters such as Ernst and Dalí. He practised 'psychic automatism', producing paintings as an unfettered stream of consciousness although he did not completely abandon methodical work and explored the uses of other media such as in set design and stained glass. Miró often described his working methods as experimental and highly spontaneous and that he was sometimes inspired by hunger-induced hallucinations and by chance movements of his paintbrush.

Miró was one of the first artists to utilise automatic drawing. For him, it was a way to step outside established traditional painting methods, and thus, with André Masson, he represented the beginning of Surrealism as an art movement.

Miró married Pilar Juncosa in Palma, Mallorca on October 12th 1929.

From the beginning of the Spanish Civil War (1936–1939), Miró was unable to return home to Spain each summer. Although his work was not particularly political, that of his Surrealist contemporaries was and he considered it prudent to stay in France, only returning to Spain in May 1940. By the late 1940s, he was able to resume his visits to Paris.

Miró spent significant time in New York in the 1940s, where he and other Surrealist émigrés inspired the imaginations of emerging Abstract Expressionists.

In 1959, André Breton asked Miró to represent Spain in The Homage to Surrealism exhibition. In 1974, Miró and Josep Royo jointly created a tapestry for the World Trade Center in New York City. It was one of the most expensive works of art lost during the terrorist attacks on September 11th 2001. Miró also created more than 250 illustrated books known as 'Livres d' Artiste'.

In the final decades of his life, Miró produced hundreds of ceramics, including the *Wall of the Moon* and *Wall of the Sun* at the UNESCO building in Paris. Towards the end of his life, Miró recorded his most radical ideas which explored the concepts of four-dimensional painting and gas sculpture.

Miró died at his home in Palma, Mallorca on December 25th 1983 and rests in the Montjuïc Cemetery in Barcelona. Two museums are dedicated to his work, the Fundació Joan Miró in Barcelona and the Fundació Pilar i Joan Miró in his adoptive city of Palma. Since his death, the number and size of exhibitions and retrospectives devoted to Miró are an indication of the international acclaim that has grown steadily in recent decades.

André Masson (1896–1987)

André Masson was a French painter, sculptor, illustrator, designer and writer. He was born on January 4th 1896 at Balagny-sur-Thérain, Oise near Paris. The family moved to Lille and then Brussels where he grew up. At the age of eleven, he was admitted to study at the Académie Royale des Beaux-Arts in Brussels, under the guidance of Constant Montald, whose methods of mixing glue with water and paint pigment were a lasting influence. He later attended the Ecole des Beaux-Arts in Paris from 1912 to 1914. He visited Italy in 1914 to study fresco painting and also to Switzerland where he became fascinated and affected by the writings of Frederich Nietzsche.

He fought for France during World War I and was seriously injured in the chest causing him to spend months in military and psychiatric hospitals. These experiences were responsible for the violent imagery that ran through his work for the rest of his life. Discharged in 1917, he met and married Odette Cabalé and they moved first to Paris and then to the South of France from 1919–1922. They returned to Paris in 1923 where he met Joan Miró, André Breton, and others. The group experimented with altered states of consciousness, smoking hashish and opium or going for long periods without food and sleep. They believed that it would free their art from conscious control in order to summon inspiration from the subconscious mind.

Masson's first solo exhibition was held at the Galerie Simon, Paris in 1923. His automatic drawings in pen and ink that followed are often accepted as the turning point away from Dadaism because they point to the unconscious mind as being the inspiration behind the works although the English artist Austin Osman Spare wrote about the subject as early as 1913. From 1924 to 1929, he was an active member of the Surrealist movement although many of the Surrealists' automatic drawings were only partially drawn from the unconscious. Once a recognisable form appeared to manifest itself, they would often consciously intervene to make the image understandable or more acceptable. André Masson acknowledged that his own drawings were a two-stage process along these lines. From 1926, he also created a random element in some of his work by sprinkling and pasting glue on to a canvas and then scattering sand across the surface. Then he would quickly cover the canvas with paint to produce chance patterns of brushwork and colour.

He divorced Odette in 1929 and married Rose Makles in 1932.

By the end of the 1920s, he felt constricted by automatic drawing. He left the Surrealist movement to adopt a more structured style and many of his works possessed erotic or violent themes. He moved to Spain in 1934 but the atrocities of the Spanish Civil War (1935–1939) greatly disturbed him. His experiences were reflected in a number of his paintings from the period and he returned to France in 1936 and reconciled with André Breton and the Surrealists.

When Germany occupied France in World War 2, the Nazis condemned Masson's work as degenerate. He left France and found shelter on the French island of Martinique before seeking refuge in the United States in 1941, as did many of the Surrealists. Whilst living in Connecticut, his work had a profound effect on the American abstract expressionists, particularly Jackson Pollock. In 1943, Masson finally broke his long friendship with André Breton although he continued to experiment with Surrealism.

At the end of the war in 1945, he returned to France and settled in Aix-en-Provence in 1947. There, he painted landscapes of mountains and waterfalls for several years before producing abstract pictures.

In 1965, he was commissioned to paint the ceiling of the Odéon-Théâtre de L'Europe in Paris and although he completed the work, the project proved to be very demanding and it was his last major work. Masson died on October 28th 1987 at his home in Paris.

Salvador Dalí (1904–1989)

Salvador Dalí was born on May 11th 1904 in Figueres, Spain. He was one of the greatest ever Surrealist artists and was renowned for his eccentric behaviour and bizarre images. He joined the Surrealists in 1929 and created several automatic drawings but this was just one of his many experimental methods. His main inspiration was taken from Freud's writings on the subconscious. Unlike the Surrealists, who created art through automatism and random chance, Dalí tended towards a dreamlike state whilst creating his abstract paintings, employing imagery derived from his dreams and fantasies. He described his state of mind as being 'paranoiac critical.' He created a huge body of work including *The Persistence of Memory* (1931), *Lobster Telephone* (1936), the *Mae West Lips Sofa* (1937), *Christ of Saint John of the Cross* (1951), and including his only novel *Hidden* Faces (1944). He collaborated with the director Luis Buñuel on two surrealist films, *Un Chien Andalou* (1929) and *L'Age d'Or* (1930), and created the dream sequence in Hitchcock's *Spellbound* (1945). Dalí's decision to support the Franco regime prompted Pablo Picasso to terminate their long friendship. He often avoided paying restaurant bills by creating a drawing on the cheques, knowing that the restaurant would never cash them.

Plagued by ill health for the last eight years of his life, Dalí died of heart failure on January 23rd 1989 in Figueres. There are two major museums devoted to his work, in Figueres and in St Petersburg, Florida.

Wolfgang Paalen (1905–1959)

Wolfgang Paalen was an Austrian-Mexican painter, sculptor, and art theorist. He was born on July 22nd 1905 in Vienna, Austria. He was a member of the Abstraction-Création group from 1933 to 1935 then joined the Surrealist movement in Paris and was one of its notable exponents until 1942. In the mid-1940s, his work influenced the beginnings of Abstract Expressionism. Paalen created several notable automatic drawings in Paris in the late 1940s but he is better known for creating the technique of fumage where evocative patterns are generated from the soot and smoke of a burning candle. He also wrote poetry and three theatre plays. Paalen also had a passion for archaeology and explored the ancient Mesoamerican Olmec culture in Mexico. On September 25th 1959, his ongoing depression drove him to commit suicide in Taxco, Mexico. His works rarely come up for sale.

Francis Bacon (1909–1992)

Bacon, a descendant of the philosopher Francis Bacon (1561–1626), was born on October 28th 1909 in Dublin. He did not paint seriously until his late thirties. His influences included Fritz Lang's *Metropolis* (1927), the works of Matthias Grünewald, and the scene with the terrified nurse on the Odessa steps from Sergei Eisenstein's *Battleship Potemkin* (1925) which inspired the recurring motif of screaming mouths in many of his works.

Although associated with automatism, he thought himself to be a medium for chance and mining the subconscious was of no great interest to him.

His work is more closely allied to Surrealism, particularly the triptych paintings titled *Crucifixion*. The first of these, commissioned by his patron Eric Hall, launched Bacon's career as a serious artist in 1933 but it was poorly received and this caused him to abandon painting for nearly ten years. Its sombre, monochrome palette contrasted strongly with the brighter colours in his second triptych *Three Studies for Figures at the Base of a Crucifixion*. Released in 1944, it confirmed his reputation as a bleak illustrator of the human condition and a prominent post-war artist.

Bacon preferred to paint from photographs of his friends and a snapshot of Eric Hall in the park led to one of his most important paintings, *Figure in a Landscape* (1945). His best-known work, *Painting* (1946), soon followed.

He died in Madrid on April 28th 1992 from pneumonia allied to asthma.

Bacon's triptych *Three Studies of Lucian Freud* (1969) realised $158.2 million at Christies New York in November 2013 and remains one of the most expensive works of art ever sold.

Jackson Pollock (1912–1956)

Paul Jackson Pollock was born on January 28th 1912 in Cody, Wyoming and grew up in Arizona and California.

He was an influential and radical American painter, a major figure in the abstract expressionist movement, and one of the few American painters to be recognized during his lifetime. His main influences derived from the works of Pablo Picasso, Joan Miró, Janet Sobel, and Wolfgang Paalen.

In 1929, he moved to New York City where he and his brother Charles studied under Thomas Hart Benton at the Art Students League. Benton would be a strong influence in the early years of Pollock's art career as were the Mexican muralists José Clemente Orozco and Diego Rivera.

During the Great Depression of the 1930s, he was desperately poor, frequently ill, and troubled by alcoholism. In spite of this, he managed to take part in the Federal Art Project from 1935 to 1943. The FAP was one of several government sponsored art programs to provide work relief for artists.

At the age of 31, the Art of This Century gallery gave Pollock his first one-man show and over the next twelve years his work was shown at eleven further exhibitions.

In 1945, he married the artist Lee Krasner (1908–1984) but by 1956 their relationship had faltered owing to his constant battle with alcoholism and an extra marital affair with Ruth Kligman.

In the years following World War 2, a new art movement surfaced that became known as Abstract Expressionism. Jackson Pollock made a huge impact and in the mid-1940s, he introduced his legendary 'drip paintings'. Abandoning the easel, Pollock preferred to fix an unstretched canvas to the wall or the floor where he could walk around it and work from all sides and angles, allowing the paint to drip from the paint can. He often used ordinary household paint and added to his images using trowels or knives rather than the traditional paintbrush. Sometimes the paint was just flung on the canvas in a frenetic style and his supplementary work often employed a heavy impasto using things such as sand and broken glass. His avant-garde style appalled some art critics who dubbed him 'Jack the Dripper'. He had been possibly introduced to 'paint pouring' in 1936 by the Mexican painter David Alfaro Siqueiros (1896–1974) or by Max Ernst (1891–1976) who also used paint dripped from a moving can. Ernst was married to one of Pollock's most vital patrons, Peggy Guggenheim.

His coverage of the whole canvas led to his technique being called 'All Over Painting'. It was also classed as 'Action Painting' when the American critic Harold Rosenberg (1906–1978) coined the term in 1952. Action Painting soon triggered a response in Europe and led to the emergence of new art movements including Tachisme and Art Informel.

In 1946, Pollock started using synthetic resin-based paints called alkyd enamels, an unfamiliar medium at the time.

Many of his artworks displayed no areas of any clear focus or identity. His most notable paintings were made between 1947 and 1950 and his first major exhibition ran from 1948 to 1951 in Paris and Europe but at the height of his fame he unexpectedly gave up the drip style.

Action Painting had associations with the Surrealists, being related to the artist's own emotional state. Automatism played a part in Pollock's Abstract Expressionism and his encounter with automatic drawing and thence to automatic painting allowed him to liberate the unconscious images in his imagination. He had previously experimented with automatic poetry in 1942 in company with Lee Krasner and other artists.

Pollock's action painting was similar to automatic painting and to some degree, automatism played a part in his work. Pollock himself stated 'The source of my painting is the Unconscious. I approach painting the same way I approach drawing, that is, directly, with no preliminary studies. When I am painting, I am not much aware of what is taking place; it is only after that I see what I have done.'

Around 1948, Pollock ceased giving titles to his works in order that the viewer should look at his paintings for what they were rather than have any preconceived ideas about them. After 1951, his paintings were darker in colour but none of them were sold when shown at the Betty Parsons Gallery in New York and he returned to a more colourful and figurative format.

In 1955, Pollock painted his last two paintings, *Scent* and *Search*. He did no painting in 1956, confining himself to a few sand cast sculptures with rough textured surfaces.

On August 11th 1956, Pollock died in a car crash near his home in Springs, New York while he was driving under the influence of alcohol. One of his passengers, Edith Metzger, was also killed but his mistress, Ruth Kligman, survived. His widow, Lee Krasner, remained loyal, managing his estate and maintaining his reputation in the art world until she died.

By the early 1960s, Action Painting had shifted focus owing to criticism of its irrationality and is now better known as Gestural Abstraction. Perhaps Pollock's biggest legacy is the proliferation of other art movements that emerged after Action Painting including Conceptual art, Performance art, and Installation art.

In February 2016, David Geffen sold Jackson Pollock's 1948 painting *Number 17A* to Kenneth C Griffin for US$200 million.

Pierre Gauvreau (1922–2011)

Pierre Gauvreau was born on August 23rd 1922 in Montréal, Canada and studied at the École des Beaux-Arts de Montréal. He was a member of the Les Automatistes movement in Canada. Gauvreau was heavily influenced by the Surrealists and automatism and began creating abstract art, including the use of automatic drawing as a means of expression. He was a signatory to the Surrealist Manifesto *Refus Global* which he typed and printed himself. By the mid-1950s, he was working in television as a writer, director, and producer and was known for his popular series *Le Temps d'une Paix* (Time for Peace) which ran for 135 episodes between 1980 and 1986. He did no painting between 1965 and 1975. He died in Montréal on April 7th 2011.

Ellsworth Kelly (1923–2015)

Ellsworth Kelly was an American painter, sculptor, and printmaker. He was born on May 31st 1923 in Newburgh, New York and grew up in New Jersey where he developed his instinct for colour and form and his love of wild birds. As an artist, he rejected the notion of art as self-expression.

He attended public school where the art classes cultivated artistic imagination and a teacher encouraged him to develop his talent. From 1941, Kelly studied at Brooklyn's Pratt Institute until he was drafted into the U.S. Army on New Year's Day 1943 when he was assigned, as were many other artists, to the 603rd Engineers Camouflage Battalion. He served with a 1,100 man deception unit known as the Ghost Army, which used inflatable tanks and trucks etc to simulate military activity. After the war, the benefits of the 1944 G.I. Bill allowed him to study from 1946–1947 at the School of the Museum of Fine Arts, Boston and then at the École des Beaux-Arts in Paris.

He had heard Max Beckmann's talk on the French artist Paul Cézanne in 1948 and moved to Paris soon afterwards. He spent six years in Paris from 1948 to 1954, where he was influenced by Henri Matisse, Pablo Picasso, and Piet Mondrian and they influenced the abstract forms he used in his work. He visited the studios of Constantin Brâncusi, Georges Vantongerloo, and Jean Arp, with whom he struck up a close friendship.

In 1950, a close friend from Boston, Ralph Coburn, introduced Kelly to the surrealist technique of automatic drawing and the game of 'Exquisite Corpse'. Although not directly linked to Surrealism, Kelly adopted the method of making an image without looking at the sheet of paper or whilst blindfolded. Many of his drawings were created by using the method of automatism.

In the 1940s and 1950s, Kelly was a pioneer of 'hard-edge painting' whereby abrupt transitions are found between areas of bold colour and by May 1949, he had already made his first abstract paintings. Kelly became fascinated with 'transcribing' the designs and structures of random objects such as seaweed and window frames. In spite of having a one-man show at Galerie Arnaud in 1951, his artworks did not sell. Nearly penniless, Kelly got a job under the 1948 Marshall Plan as a caretaker in a Paris office. In 1952, the influence of Monet's later works inspired him to start working in very large formats and from then on, he worked in an exclusively abstract mode. By 1953, Kelly's French had not improved and he had sold only one painting, leading to his eviction from his studio.

When he returned to America in the summer of 1954, he had accumulated a large amount of original art and begun work on the colour panel paintings that would make him famous. By the late 1950s, his paintings often assumed non-rectilinear formats and in the 1960s he started working with irregularly angled canvases. In May 1956, Kelly had his first solo New York City exhibition at the Betty Parsons gallery. Although he is renowned for his paintings, he also created sculpture throughout his career. In 1958, Kelly produced one of his first wood sculptures, a modest wall relief in elm. He made 30 sculptures in wood during his career. From 1959 onwards, he created freestanding folded sculptures in paper and card. In the mid-1960s, he began printmaking in earnest and produced his *Suite of Twenty-Seven Lithographs*. The *Suite of Plant Lithographs* grew to 72 prints and countless drawings of foliage. His *Purple/Red/Gray/Orange* (1988) is eighteen feet in length and is possibly the largest single-sheet lithograph ever made. In 1970, Kelly left New York City to live in Spencertown and in 1984 he was joined there by his partner, photographer Jack Shear. In 2005, they moved to an 1815 Colonial house which they shared until Kelly's death in 2015. For the last fourteen years of his life, Kelly occupied a huge studio of 20,000 square feet in Spencertown. In 1973, Kelly embarked upon a series of large-scale outdoor sculptures. He abandoned painted surfaces and utilised plain steel, aluminum or bronze in his construction of totem-like structures which were freestanding and measured up to fifteen feet in height. Of similar magnitude, his wall reliefs measured more than fourteen feet in width. In the 1980s, Kelly devoted as much time and energy to his sculptures as he did to his painting, and in doing so produced more than 80 of his 140 sculptures.

During his career, Kelly created his sculpture pieces using a series of ideas in various configurations. They might have started life as a drawing, then modified to create a print which was converted into a freestanding piece, which was then made into a sculpture.

Ellsworth Kelly died in Spencertown, New York on December 27th 2015, aged 92. Jack Shear now serves as the director of the Ellsworth Kelly Foundation. Kelly received many awards between 1963 and 2013 and since 1973, his work has been recognized in numerous retrospective exhibitions. Today, his work is in many public collections, including those in Paris, Madrid, New York, and London. The actress Gwyneth Paltrow is a notable private collector of his work. Kelly executed many public commissions including a mural for the UNESCO headquarters in Paris in 1969 and *Berlin Totem*, a 40 feet stainless-steel sculpture, in the courtyard of the U.S. Embassy in Berlin in 2008. On May 31st 2019, the United States Postal Service issued a set of ten stamps in honour of Kelly's career.

William Anastasi (1933–)

William Anastasi was born on August 11th 1933 in Philadelphia. He is an American artist considered to be a pioneer of conceptual and minimal Art in the 1960s. Although the practice of automatic drawing is not of paramount importance to him, his methods appear to be clearly influenced by automatism. His 'Subway' series consists of drawings that were made while he was walking or travelling on the New York subway and not looking at the paper. In 2007, at the White Box Gallery in New York, he and Lucio Pozzi made dozens of drawings over eight hours whilst blindfolded. Although not directly connected with automatic drawing, many of his art practices draw upon the subconscious in the creation of his work.

Freddy Flores Knistoff (1948–)

Freddy Flores Knistoff was born on October 10th 1948 in Viña del Mar, Chile. He is a painter and producer of artist's books. He also composes experimental poetry and has lived in Amsterdam since 1985. In 1991, along with the Dutch painter Rik Lina, he co-founded the Collective Automatic Painting of Amsterdam (CAPA), an international and experimental group of artists. Through this movement, they influenced other artists in the use of automatic painting. Initially interested in the development of automatism itself, the group now practises collaborative art where more than one artist may work simultaneously on a single painting. Knistoff has connections with the FLUXUS and Phases international art movements.

Printed in Great Britain
by Amazon